What Must a Student's Manual Achieve?

When we first talked about writing this student's manual we asked ourselves "What must the student's manual achieve?" After considerable discussion we outlined these objectives:

1. Immediate specific: The student's manual must give each student who uses it a better chance of success in the course than students who do not use it.

2. Immediate specific: The student's manual must lead each user to a better understanding of psychology than will occur without it.

3. Immediate general: The student's manual must show each student how to improve his or her learning ability and studying efficiency in all courses.

4. Long range: The student's manual must enhance self-development. It must help each student take control of his or her life-long self-education and personal development.

Our next question--"How can these objectives be reached?"--guided the development of this book.

Section I "How to Be a More Successful Student and Still Keep Your Friends" is based on practical experience rather than theory and provides clear guidelines on how to be more successful in school.

In Section II we present a step-by-step program which, if followed, will help insure your success in the course and help you develop good mental habits while acquiring a solid understanding of psychology.

In Section III we provide sample questions, checklists, and tests necessary to the program described in Section II. Each of our chapters contains questions intended to challenge your mind, suggestions for further reading, chapter objectives, and action projects designed to show you how to do things with psychology. Most of the action projects will take you away from your desk and involve you in exploring human behavior in the world around you.

The chapter objectives are included in the <u>Student Manual</u> and in the <u>Instructor's Manual</u> to help you focus on the important concepts for each chapter and to establish points that are primary in both the learning and teaching of introductory psychology.

The answer to our third question--"<u>How will we know if the objectives are reached?</u>"--will come partly from you. The last page of this book is a feedback sheet which we'd like you to send us with your comments.

--Al Siebert   --Tim Walter

PART I

How to Be a More Successful Student
and Still Keep Your Friends

I. How to Make It through School
   Develop Useful Habits
   Choose Some Goals
   Be Responsible for You
   Use Psychology on Yourself
   Checklist for Success

II. How to Make Studying Easier
   Plan to Score
   Eliminate Distractions
   Accept Your Humanness
   Be an Active Learner
   Write the Test
   Checklist for Success

III. How to Become More Intelligent and Be Successful in Your Classes
   Ask Intelligent Questions
   Generate Intelligent Questions
   Increase Your Reading Speed and Comprehension
   Shape Up Your Instructor
   Checklist for Success

DEVELOP USEFUL HABITS

You may have heard some talk about good study habits and poor study habits. What people are saying is that your <u>habits</u> determine whether or not you learn much during the time you spend going to school. Two students may spend the same amount of time in classes and studying, but the student with good study habits learns more and gets a better education than the student with poor study habits.

When Benjamin Franklin was 22 years old he realized the importance of habits in his life. Here is how he described his discovery in his <u>Autobiography</u>:

> It was about this time I conceived the bold and arduous project of arriving at moral perfection. I wished to live without committing any fault at any time; I would conquer all that either natural inclination, custom, or company might lead me into. As I knew, or thought I knew, what was right and wrong, I did not see why I might not always do the one and avoid the other. But I soon found I had undertaken a task of more difficulty than I had imagined. While my attention was taken up and care employed in guarding against one fault, I was often surprised by another. Habit took the advantage of inattention. Inclination was sometimes too strong for reason. I concluded at length that the mere speculative conviction that it was our interest to be completely virtuous was not sufficient to prevent our slipping, and that the contrary habits must be broken and good ones acquired and established before we can have any dependence on a steady, uniform retitude of conduct.

Franklin went on to describe the plan he worked out for acquiring the habits he knew were necessary. He would work on one habit at a time for one week at a time. He followed his plan for over two years, checking himself daily to see how well he was doing in acquiring the habits he desired. He reasoned that if he put constant mental effort into one desirable change for a week then the change should hold up during the next two weeks out of habit.

Students who want to improve need to work at acquiring habits they can count on. It isn't easy to develop new habits, but once you have them it makes life a lot easier. With good study habits you don't have to work so hard at studying.

CHOOSE SOME GOALS

From the time you were in the third grade you were asked, "What do you want to be when you grow up?" If you said <u>doctor</u>, <u>airline pilot</u>, <u>teacher</u>, or something which was definite and socially acceptable, then people were pleased. But what you told them was probably just part of a game you had to play.

The fact is, most students do not know what they want to be. They are waiting to see where life will take them and are curious about how things will turn out. When students declare a certain area of study as a major it is often done because the school requires them to do so at registration time. This situation helps explain why the motivation to study is low in many students. A goal that is forced on someone is not as motivating as a goal which is self-chosen.

The key to making it through school and learning something useful is to choose for yourself some goals that motivate you. Anything can be a goal. It might be to understand music, learn about computers, figure out how electricity works, be a writer, understand why economics is important to business and government, or find out what causes nations to fight each other.

One way to choose motivating goals is to think ahead to the time when you will be out of school on your own. What knowledge, skill, or ability could you acquire that people will pay for? What would you enjoy doing that will be of value to others? What interests, hobbies, or talents do you have now that could be turned into a worthwhile occupation?

If you don't have any goals and can't think of any that make you excited about your future you might see what your school's counseling center has to offer. It should have some interest and aptitude tests for you to take, and some trained counselors to help you figure out what you would like to do with yourself.

BE RESPONSIBLE FOR YOU

Your success in school is your responsibility. It is not the responsibility of your teachers, parents, friends, classmates, or the administrators. Your teachers will present ideas and information, but whether or not you learn anything is mostly up to you.

Many students have been conditioned by magazines, television, and movies to be passive. They expect to be entertained by the textbook or the instructor. The only writings and speakers they pay attention to are those that capture and hold their attention. If an instructor teaches in a boring way, they get turned off. They seem to expect a teacher to compete for their attention like a professional entertainer.

A student who feels responsible for getting something out of classes is active. He or she makes an effort to get some useful ideas from every instructor and is curious about what the textbooks have to offer.

Remember: The best investment you will ever make is your investment in yourself. You might lose your job or money, but no one can take your education away from you.

USE PSYCHOLOGY ON YOURSELF

Once you choose some goals for yourself and accept responsibility for your own learning, you've made a big step forward. You suddenly realize that you are in charge of your mind, your life, and your future. With this sense of responsibility comes the realization that you can start using psychology on yourself. By this we mean to purposefully use psychological principles of cause and effect to influence your development and learning. For example, if you daydream in class and look around a lot, you can help yourself pay attention better by sitting up in front--just as you would want to do at a concert or a football game.

5

If you are a slow reader, you can take a reading improvement course (most of them are free). If you waste a lot of time, you can begin associating with better students so that their habits influence you. (Benjamin Franklin did this. He organized a self-improvement "Junto." It was a carefully selected group of 12 persons, which met secretly to exchange books, give prepared talks, and discuss important ideas.)

Psychologists understand very well the principles of learning. The next section outlines many principles and conditions which you can use to improve how much you learn.

CHECKLIST FOR SUCCESS

_____ Write out a list of the study habits you would like to have and put it up someplace where you can check it frequently to see how well you are doing.
_____ Increase the meaningfulness of your schooling by choosing some goals that make you feel a sincere desire to get something out of your courses.
_____ Accept full responsibility for getting a good education.
_____ Apply psychological principles of cause and effect to yourself so that you can learn more in less time with less effort.

II. How to Make Studying Easier

Studying is not the same as reading <u>Cosmopolitan</u> or <u>Playboy</u>. Reading a textbook is not the same as reading a novel. There is a big difference between reading what interests you and reading an assignment.

Textbooks are not written to entertain you. You can't get away with reading only the parts that interest you. When it comes to studying, you must provide some of the motivation. Studying can be fun, but sometimes it is very hard work--as hard as physical labor.

Some students rely on will power to make themselves study. They grind away at their books week after week. But few can make it through the school year on will power alone. They run out of energy. They develop a helpless condition in which they may spend most of their time watching television or lying around. There is a feeling of bewilderment. You hear statements like: "I know I'm going to flunk if I don't study, but I can't even make myself open a book."

Once this condition develops it is difficult to cure, so the best approach is to prevent it. And that is what this section is all about: How to study with less effort while learning more.

PLAN TO SCORE

Ernie R. walked to his counselor's office with his head down and a disgusted look on his face. So his grades were low! So what! He was the best sophomore halfback in the conference this year.

"Come in Speedy."

Ernie smiled to himself. "Speed-E" is how the headlines read. "Do you have any idea why I asked you to come in?"

"Grades?"

"Right. The way things look you may be on academic probation next fall."

Ernie gritted his teeth. "That means no football."

"Right, and it means you aren't getting much out of college."

"I try, but I don't have time."

"The coaches say you have been lifting weights and running with the cross-country team this spring, but that doesn't take more time than what other students are doing. You have the time. What are you doing with it?"

Ernie shrugged his shoulders.

"Your English grade is very low. When do you study English?"

"When I can."

"How about sociology?"

"When I can."

"Tell me how the coach runs training camp."

Ernie brightened up. "He has this schedule every week. We do calesthenics, run wind sprints, pass and kick, learn plays, block and tackle, scrimmage..."

"Right, and if you didn't train like that, could you win your football games?"

Ernie made a face. These intellectual nuts sure were dumb. "No way."

"Right. So if you are going to score in courses, what might you do?"

"Have a training camp?"

"Sort of. How about a weekly training schedule for yourself?"

Ernie looked out the window and nodded. Maybe this guy wasn't so dumb.

"Here's a blank schedule sheet. Take this pencil and let's work out a weekly study schedule for you. Then you can put it up in your room just as the coach does with his schedule at training camp."

One of the best helps for any student is a study schedule. Start by purchasing a monthly calendar with spaces you can fill in with exam dates and times when papers and projects are due. Marking exam times helps keep you aware of what your studying is leading up to. Next, fill in all the times you plan to go to meetings, concerts or shows, take trips, and so on. Now you are ready to make up a weekly schedule of your classes and the hours during which you plan to study. A weekly schedule gives you a clear picture of what you are doing with your time and helps you spot an extra hour or two during the day you can use for studying, so that your entire evening is free to do what you want.

A schedule seems to have motivating effects. By knowing that you have an hour on Thursday morning reserved for studying, you are mentally prepared to spend that hour studying.

The weekly schedule blank on the next page has been printed so that you can make copies of it and post it in your room. But don't fill one out right now--we have something else to say about study periods later on. First, we want you to look your room over.

Weekly Schedule

	Monday	Tuesday	Wednesday	Thursday	Friday	Saturday	Sunday
7-8							
8-9							
9-10							
10-11							
11-12							
12-1							
1-2							
2-3							
3-4							
4-5							
5-6							
6-7							
7-8							
8-9							
9-10							
10-11							
11-12							

ELIMINATE DISTRACTIONS

Visual Distractions

Sue M. is like most students. She has created a comfy nest for herself in her room. It is made up of posters, ribbons, signs, photographs, letters, mugs with pencils, an old bottle, hats, her high-school yearbooks, and several rocks. All these things have special meaning for her.

And that's the trouble. When she is studying, her mind is easily distracted from her textbook. The rock she notices out of the corner of her eye reminds her of a weekend at the beach with a special person. The next thing she knows she's spent the next 30 minutes daydreaming.

If you study at your desk, you will be able to keep your mind on your studies more easily by keeping your desk free of memory things. Some students carry this too far, however. Some rooms look like monastic cells with nothing but bare walls and one small light on the desk. While the bare walls make sense, the one small light does not. A person may get more studying done, but his eyes may not last very long.

For minimum eyestrain your room should be well illuminated with the main light source off to your side. A light directly behind or in front of you reflects off the glossy pages of your textbooks. This constant glare tires your eyes more quickly than indirect lighting. If you can't shift the lamp, shift your desk, placing it so that no portion of the bulb shines directly into your eyes. A strong light source pulls your eye to look at it. The constant strain of trying to avoid looking and of trying to read immediately after accidentally looking causes eye fatigue.

Auditory Distractions

Quiet Hours in dorms rarely work as well as the rule makers hope. Distracting sounds still interrupt studying. Doors slam, phones ring, horns honk, planes fly over, and people move around. In fact, the quieter the study area, the more these sounds become distracting.

Steady background sounds "mask" distracting noises. One way to apply this knowledge is to play your radio or stereo softly while you study. Your purpose will be to create a steady background of "noise" to mask occasional sounds. Experiment with stations or records until you find what works best for you. FM radio stations playing instrumental music are usually best. Talk shows and fast-talking disc jockeys are usually worse for concentration than nothing at all. Some women say turning on their hair dryers helps them study; and one student reported that he tunes his radio to a place where there is no program--he says the static keeps him from being distracted.

Territorial Distractions

"Hey Sally! Let's go over to the law library to study."
"Right on, Marge! I might see that law student I met in the student union last week!"

Some students study in the library to get away from their rooms. It's a good idea even when no library reading must be done, because the atmosphere lends itself to studying.

There are those students, both men and women, who use library time as a combination advertising and scouting trip. There's nothing wrong with this. It's just that a student who goes for this reason should not be surprised to get little studying done.

The problem is that whenever we enter a new territory our senses are drawn to the environment. We automatically scan new surroundings. We check the walls, floor, and ceiling. We look at the lights, decorations, and furnishings. We look at the people, wonder about certain sounds, and have to adjust to the feeling of a new chair. Every time you go to a new place this happens. It is as automatic as the way a cat checks out new surroundings before it can settle down.

If you are serious about studying, pick out one spot and always study there. Preparatory set and place habits shorten your warm-up time, and sensory adaptation allows you to concentrate on your studies better.

ACCEPT YOUR HUMANNESS

Concentration Span

Karen H. is a sophomore English major. During the summer she decided that when she came back to college she would study three hours every night without interruptions. She put a sign on her door:

Off Limits from 7 to 10 P.M.

KEEP OUT

THIS MEANS YOU!

Is she getting lots of studying done? Yes and no. She has the ability to keep her body sitting at her desk for several hours at a time, but she has a problem she hardly knows exists.

While her eyes are looking at her book her mind takes breaks. She sometimes finishes reading several pages and then realizes she has no idea of what she has read. She was daydreaming while she was reading!

Does Karen need more will power? No. She needs to accept the idea that she is a human being. She needs to accept the idea that there are certain limitations on what the human mind should be expected to do.

The way to make studying easy is to start with what you can do now and build on that. On the average, how long can you study before your mind slips off into something else? 45 minutes? 25 minutes? 10 minutes? Most freshmen and sophomores find that they can concentrate on a textbook about 10-15 minutes before starting to daydream.

Let's say that you find that your average concentration span is about 12 minutes. Now the question is, What would you like it to be? 30 minutes? 45 minutes?

Whatever goal you set for yourself make certain you allow for your humanness. Be realistic. Set a goal that you can reach with reasonable effort and give yourself enough time to reach it. As a rough guideline you might aim for a time span of 15 minutes by the end of your freshman year; 25 minutes--sophomore year; 35--junior year; 45 minutes--senior year. Graduate students should be able to study for about an hour without losing their concentration.

Mandatory Breaks

Once you have determined your concentration span, set up your study schedule so that you take a brief break after each study segment and a long break about once an hour. If you do this you will find that you can start and return to your studies much more easily than before.

In fact, you will find the end of a study segment coming so quickly you will be tempted to continue. Don't do it. Keep your agreement with yourself. When you promise to get up and take a quick break after 12 minutes, then do so. Do not allow yourself to study more than the alotted time.

A look at the record of most students shows why it is necessary to take these breaks even when you don't want to. With segmented study hours studying is easier than expected. But after a while the old ways of studying creep back in.

What happens? The critical point comes when you reach the end of study segments and find yourself so interested in the material you decide to keep on. If you do this, then your mind seems to say: "I can't trust you. You promised me a break after each 14 minutes, but after I fulfilled my part you kept me working."

When you promise your mind a break after 12 or 14 minutes keep your word. No matter how much you want to keep on, make yourself take a break. Get up and stretch. Walk out to get a drink of water or a breath of fresh air before starting the next study segment.

Avoiding Retroactive and Proactive Inhibition

Mark is carrying a full load in school--English, biology, chemistry, psychology, and Spanish. He studies quite a bit in the evenings and does pretty well. He set up a schedule for himself. He asks questions to work up interest. And he takes breaks fairly often. But when he tries to recall what he's covered in an evening he has trouble doing so.

Is Mark a slow learner? Probably not. The reason for his memory problem can be found in his study schedule. His evenings look like this:

	Mon.	Tue.	Wed.	Thur.	Fri.	Sat.	Sun.
7-8	Eng.	biol.	chem.	psych.			Span.
8-9							
9-10							

Mark's memory problem exists because he spends from 2-3 hours on one subject. When a person learns one set of facts and then goes on to learn a similar set of facts, the second set will interfere with his memory of the first and the first will interfere with the second. The more similar material a person tries to learn at one time, the worse his memory will be.

How can you avoid this when you have lots of material to study? The best way is to mix your study hours with dissimilar material. To avoid the effects of retroactive and proactive inhibition you should not devote all of one evening to one subject. Switch subjects every hour or so, and always try to make your new subject as different as possible from what you have just finished. That way your mind can be assimilating one topic while you are reading about another. Mark did much better when he loosened up his schedule and began a study schedule like this:

	Mon.	Tue.	Wed.	Thur.	Fri.	Sat.	Sun.
7-8	Eng.	psych.	biol.	chem.			Span.
8-9	biol.	chem.	Span.	Eng.			psych.
9-10	Span.	Eng.	psych.	biol.			chem.

While Mark's schedule shows that he knows how to mix dissimilar subjects he still may not be applying other principles of learning. Research shows that material learned by rote memory is retained better if immediately followed by sleep. Insightful learning can occur at any time and is not vulnerable to what follows immediately. This means that subjects like Spanish and chemistry will tend to be remembered better if studied immediately before bedtime.

BE AN ACTIVE LEARNER

Reading is not studying. You can improve the amount of material remembered by being an active learner. After reading a chapter in the textbook, close the book and outline as many of the main points you remember as possible.

The first time you try this you will be in for a surprise. It takes much more effort to recall material than to recognize it. Learning material so well that you can recall it is the most thorough method of learning. If you find this too difficult to do by yourself, then try arranging discussion sessions with other students. Quiz each other on the material while discussing the importance of the topics covered. The more you question, write, recall, and talk about the material, the better your learning will be. (Suggestions on how to do this will be covered in the section on "How to Become More Intelligent and Be Successful in Your Classes.")

WRITE THE TEST

"Hi Speedy, how's it going?"
Ernie shook his head.
"What are you worried about?"
"I do the schedule, but they ask questions I don't know."
"The exams catch you by surprise. Right?"
Ernie nodded.
"How does the defensive unit prepare for a foot ball game?"
"We run our offense the way the other team runs theirs. We study films and run their plays against our defense."
"Right. So how about doing that before exams?"
"Run plays?"
"Same thing. Get each instructor to tell you as much as possible about what the test will be like. Get copies of old tests to see what facts and ideas the instructor likes to emphasize. Each teacher has favorite points he likes to make just as each team has favorite plays it likes to run. Find out if the questions will be multiple choice, fill in, or essay. Then pretend you are the instructor. Make up an exam just like the one he will give you. Or, better yet, get someone else in the class to give you a test like the instructor's."
Ernie looked away and nodded. It might work. With one more

good effort it might work. He looked back at the counselor for a
moment, grinned, and headed off to his room.

CHECKLIST FOR SUCCESS

_____ Outline a weekly study schedule for yourself.
_____ Keep your study desk free of memory things.
_____ Play soft music to mask distracting sounds.
_____ Arrange good lighting.
_____ When you go to the library try to study in the same place.
_____ Determine your concentration span and set up study segments
       geared to your current level.
_____ Take short breaks after study segments and a long break each
       hour.
_____ Avoid studying one subject all evening. Change to a different
       subject every hour or so.
_____ Prepare for exams by trying to write questions as similar as
       possible to what the instructor will write.

III. How to Become More Intelligent
and Be Successful in Your Classes

     Most of us believe we are intelligent people, especially those of
us in academic communities. A favorite pastime of many students and
instructors who gather in classrooms, offices, coffee houses, and dormitory rooms is to discuss that highly controversial subject: "What is an
intelligent person?" Is such a person creative? A wise decision-maker?
A person who thinks for himself? If we choose to go beyond these
subjective definitions--all of which are certainly on target--we find
one predominant characteristic. An intelligent person can ask and answer
important questions related to his or her field of interest.
     If we lean back in our chairs and analyze what a successful student
must do, it is clear that such a student must ask and answer intelligent
questions. This will be done when writing papers, reading books, talking
in discussion groups, making speeches, and certainly while taking tests.
Think of your textbook. It is a lot of answers to a lot of questions.
Your professors and teaching fellows spend a good deal of time looking
in texts to find questions they may ask you in class or on tests. Think
of the notes you take. Are they anything more than a set of answers to
questions? Your instructors have carefully analyzed important books,
speeches, films, and other documents to generate a body of information
which they present to you in lectures. The final task for you is to
answer important questions regarding things you have been told in class,
read in books, or watched in films.
     Let's look at a simple and highly effective set of learning tech-
niques which have been developed over the past 15 years at the University
of Michigan. Several thousand students who used these techniques found
that when they learned to ask and answer intelligent questions, they

became highly successful students, saved hundreds of hours in studying and preparing for courses, and were able to spend more time going to movies, watching TV, chatting with friends, going on weekend trips, going to protest rallies, and generally leading the "good life."

If these things interest you, then let's spend a little more time discussing how you can learn these techniques. One thing we promise is that you will achieve your academic goals with a great deal of pleasure and far less pain than you have known in the past. We must sound one word of caution. This may require you to change many of your old habits. Such changes are sometimes difficult or painful. Why? Well, when you are used to a standard set of procedures to accomplish your goals you often become comfortable with them and resist change. If you try the new techniques, you'll have a tendency to go back to the old behaviors. These old behaviors will accomplish your goals to a degree, but with the same pain and tremendous number of hours that you've spent in the past. Once you become accustomed to the new techniques a lot of your old superstitious behavior about how one studies and becomes educated will fade away. You will begin getting some good feedback from professors, friends, and yourself that the new methods save time. You will achieve your goals and have time to do things you never had time for in the past. Here we go!

The Key to Studying and Becoming Intelligent

Whenever you are reading out of curiosity, allow your mind to go in any direction it wishes. Whenever you study, <u>study as though you are practicing to take a test</u>! If you don't, you are wasting your time! Remember, it's your time; so why waste it? Allowing your mind to drift in any direction it wishes is not studying.

ASK INTELLIGENT QUESTIONS

"What is an intelligent question?"
It is one:
    you would like answered.
    where by looking for the answer you learn other things which are important to you.
    your instructor is likely to ask.
    which helps you appear intelligent.

"What will good questions help you do?"
They will help you:
    determine whether you and your instructor are interested in the same things.
    focus on the important points while listening and reading.
    prepare for exams.
    determine how ready you are to take an exam.
    discriminate important from unimportant material.
    determine the important points of lectures and readings.
    influence your instructor.
    save time.

"What does a good question look like?"
It usually starts with a phrase such as:

14

Give several examples of...
Which of these is an example of...
Describe the function of...
What is significant about...
List the important...
Compare and contrast...
Interpret the following...
What is the structure of...
Identify the following...

GENERATE INTELLIGENT QUESTIONS

"How can I determine what the important questions are?"

Pretending you are the instructor and generating questions from your texts, lecture notes, and old exams.

Generating questions before you go to class and then listening to see whether other students ask the same questions or whether the instructor supplies answers to those questions.

Writing out questions to a lecture or an assignment. Then, asking your instructor if he thinks these are important questions and what other questions you should attempt to answer.

DO NOT BE AFRAID TO ASK YOUR INSTRUCTOR WHAT HE THINKS ARE IMPORTANT QUESTIONS! Most instructors are happy to tell you what they think is important. Give them a chance and they'll take a mile.

Ask your professor what goals he has for the students in his class. If you want a clear answer, you must learn to ask questions which help him clarify for himself questions he would like the class members to answer. You might ask:

"What should a student be able to do and what important questions should he be able to answer after having completed this chapter (unit, training, program, and so on)?"

"What important questions do you think we should be looking at in this unit (chapter, assignment, and so on)?"

"Could you suggest some particular articles or books which highlight the issues we will be discussing in this unit?"

"What important things should we be looking for in this particular reading (film, case study, and so on)?"

These questions should be asked in as positive a manner as possible. Students have a tendency to put instructors on the defensive. It is your job to ask the instructor in what direction the course is headed and reward him for telling you. A comment such as, "Thanks, that really clarifies things for me," is something an instructor responds to well and will increase the likelihood that you won't have to ask next time.

"How should I practice improving my ability to predict and answer exam questions?"

Each day, generate and answer 1-5 good questions for each subject. Use your notes, texts, student manual, instructor, and friends to help build up your file.

Generate five good questions from each lecture. Remember, most lectures make 3-5 good points. It's not difficult to turn those statements into questions.

If there is a student or instructor's manual available, or a set of questions at the end of the chapter, compare those with ones you have generated to see how close you have come to predicting the ones the author has already given.

Each week make up a mock exam and use the questions you have generated. Take the exam under the closest possible conditions to an actual test situation. Give yourself the exact time limit allowed for the test. Upon completion, compare your answers to the text.

Ask your friends what they think are important questions and compare yours to theirs.

Periodically go through the questions you have generated to see if you can still answer them. Avoid saying to yourself, "I know the answer to that one." Verbalize or write the answer to prove to yourself how brilliant you have become.

"Is the purpose of education to learn how to answer instructors' questions?"

Yes and no! If you want to understand the experts and even go beyond them, it is important to be able to ask and answer the same questions which they believe are important. If you're realistic, you know you have to pass the requirements of the course. If you understand what your instructor wants, then you will learn a lot. If your instructor is less than adequate, then it is more a matter of meeting his criteria and later going on to better courses. There is no need to waste a lot of time in the process.

INCREASING YOUR READING SPEED AND COMPREHENSION

One of the fastest ways to save time studying is to learn how to figure out the important questions and their answers as quickly as possible.

First you should know that 80 percent of the words you read are redundant. Most words simply link key ideas together. The ideas are the answers to the questions you wish to answer.

Second, most of what you want to comprehend is already in your head. What you want to comprehend are the answers to questions you generate or find in the chapter.

Here are the steps you should go through to increase speed and comprehension:

Survey the Chapter and Generate Questions

Go to the back of the chapter to see if there is a list of questions. If so, read them, because they are the keys to comprehension. Make sure you check your study guide because it usually contains questions related to the important points the author is attempting to make.

If there is a set of questions you're ahead of the game; if not,

you soon will be. Quickly leaf through the chapter. You will be looking for titles, subtitles, illustrations, pictures, and questions placed
throughout the chapter that will give you a basic idea of what the chapter is about. Using these, formulate 5 questions which you think will
give you a good summary of what the chapter is all about.

Answer the Questions

Now take the questions you have generated and attempt to answer them
verbally. Call on prior knowledge and information you have picked up
while skimming the chapter. (Also use your ability to bull.) Try to do
this with little or no additional reading.

Generate a Summary

Using the answers you have generated, go ahead and formulate a
verbal summary. If you prefer, write it down.
If there is a summary in the chapter read it quickly to see how
many of your questions it answers and how similar it is to your summary.

Read to Confirm, Revise, or Elaborate

It is now time to confirm, revise, or elaborate your answers. Read
as fast as you can to confirm your answers, revise those which are incor-
rect or slightly off track, and elaborate when necessary.
You should now have a good understanding of the chapter. You have:

1. surveyed the chapter.
2. generated questions.
3. tried to answer them without re-reading.
4. generated a summary.
5. read selectively to answer the questions in greater detail.
6. found questions and answers which you hadn't predicted.

The End Result

You learn to predict the important questions before spending a lot
of time reading.
You learn to generate summaries and answers. You'll be pleasantly
surprised to find that you know many of the answers before you read.
All that's left is to read to confirm, elaborate, or revise.
You learn to read selectively. You read to find answers. When you
come to an answer for a question you hadn't predicted, you simply slow
down and formulate the question. When you come to material you already
know, you keep on going to find out what you don't know.

Remember: Most of the time your answers will be in titles, subtitles, or sub-headings. Occasionally you may have to read beyond these
headings for important detail. But, not with the regularity which helped
you waste a lot of time in the past while you looked for unimportant
detail.

"Why should I believe this works?"

We don't ask you to believe a word. But the data supports

these procedures. Careful analysis at the University of Michigan Reading Improvement Service and other learning centers has shown that:

Most good readers use these techniques.
Students who use the techniques improve their grades, reduce their study time significantly, and increase their speed and comprehension of the textbook.

"What are the advantages?"

You spend less time memorizing facts that you will soon forget.
You don't waste time reading and looking for things you already know.
Your preparation for tests is a continual process. By the time you get to the test you will find that you have answered most of the questions.
You focus on grasping the key concepts. Details are then much easier to remember.
You don't waste time looking for details which are unimportant to you or your instructor.
You learn to take an expert's point of view and think things out for yourself.
You learn to sit down and generate answers which you didn't think you knew. You then search for added information, which makes polished answers out of incomplete ones.
You learn to organize and structure your studying. You state your goals as questions, seek answers, achieve your goal, and move on.

"What are the disadvantages?"

It is difficult to change old study patterns. You may be accustomed to reading every word, always being afraid you're going to miss something. A new technique such as this appears to be reckless and inappropriate to scholarly learning.

"How can you reconcile these apprehensions?"

Try the techniques and look for these results:

The quality of your answers and questions will improve with practice.
The amount of time it takes you to generate questions and summaries will decrease.
The amount of time it takes to verify and improve your answers will decrease with practice.
You will be able to cover large amounts of material in far less time.
You will find that you are predicting the same questions as your instructors, texts, and questions on old exams.
You will find that the summaries you generate come closer to those of the author with practice. Thus, you won't need to spend a lot of time generating summaries, and can focus on simply answering questions.

These techniques are based on several well-established learning principles.

18

When you learn material under conditions which are similar to those under which you will be tested, there is a greater likelihood that you will remember that material.

People learn meaningful material faster than they memorize unrelated or nonsense information.

Learning new material is easier when you associate it with familiar material.

"How should I begin?"

Each week, count those questions and answers you have generated from past exams, lecture notes, texts, student and instructor guides, and your classmates. Keep a graph of the number of questions and answers for each class.

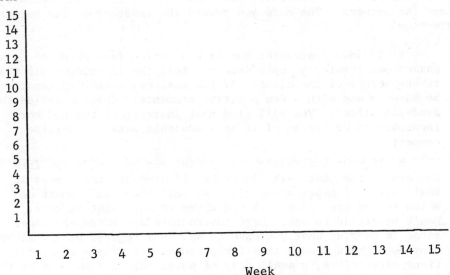

SHAPE UP YOUR INSTRUCTOR

Many students soon realize that college professors are not usually trained to be effective teachers. Contrary to public opinion you needn't live with this. Students needn't spend their time discussing the incompetency of this professor or that teaching fellow. Rather, they may use several simple strategies for shaping their instructor's behavior. What you really want is to receive a clear definition of what your instructor wants and how he expects you to get there. The student who is timid and afraid to take an active role in improving his instructor's performance can expect nothing more than mediocre classes. To get good teaching you must actively work to teach your instructors what effective teaching is all about.

A Strategy for Teaching Your Professor How to Teach

You can influence what the instructor teaches you by asking for information about important questions you want answered. Talk your questions over with other students before class so that the instructor will see that more than one student is interested. If the instructor cannot answer the question immediately, ask if he or she will put some time into it during a future class. Most instructors are pleased to have students ask for information. Try it! Try asking questions such as:

"What is your position regarding_____?"

"How does this position _____ differ from _____?"

"The text makes this distinction, but it is rather unclear, could you clarify the point about _____?"

"I am not sure how this theory is related to this problem. Could you tell us how it does?"

"What do you think about _____'s statement that _____?"

When your instructor does something which you define as good teaching, let him know you appreciate it. Rewards for effectual teaching are few and far between. The more you reward the instructor, the better the instruction!

   a. If your instructor has an evaluation form which he or she passes out regularly, make sure you tell the instructor all the strong points of the class. If you must say something negative, be sure to end with a few positive comments. This is called the sandwich effect. You will find that instructors respond more favorably to criticism if it is sandwiched between positive comments.

   b. If your instructor only passes out an evaluation form at the end of the year, ask him or her if students could pass in small slips of paper after class so that they can comment on which things are going well and where things might improve. Don't be afraid to ask. Most instructors are extremely interested in hearing what you have to say on a regular basis. Although many don't have enough time for personal interviews or conversations after class, a small slip of paper that can be read at the instructor's convenience will result in a good feedback system.

   c. Pay close attention to what your instructor is saying in class. When he or she is doing things which you define as effective teaching be very attentive, nod, even smile. An instructor's performance is determined by the attention received from the students. When student reactions indicate approval for certain behaviors you will find these behaviors increasing in frequency.

   d. When your instructor is doing something which you define as ineffective teaching (lecturing about trivia, telling personal stories, and so on) act disinterested. It is important that you not reward the instructor for ineffectiveness. Your disinterest must be subtle. Once he or she gets back on track begin to look interested, nod, and smile. You'll be surprised how well instructors respond to your attention.

Remember, it is your job to let your instructor know when he or she has done a good job. If you don't, nobody else will, and you will suffer for it.

CHECKLIST FOR SUCCESS

Here is a list of guidelines which will help you monitor both your studying and your success at implementing these learning strategies:

_____ Generate questions from lectures, texts, summaries, student manuals, old tests, and discussion sessions with your friends.
_____ Ask your instructor what goals he or she has for the students in class.
_____ Keep a weekly record of the number of questions and answers you generate for each class.
_____ Practice reading to answer the questions you have generated.
_____ Practice answering the questions you find in your student manual.
_____ Practice taking tests under conditions as similar as possible to those under which the test will be given.
_____ Practice writing summaries of chapters.
_____ Give your instructor continual feedback on the things he or she is doing well.

One Final Tip

It is not necessary to play the "suffering student" game. Learning can be pleasant and studying for exams can be handled efficiently by applying the principles we've just discussed. If you prepare well for exams then the night before each exam you can relax and do one more very helpful thing. Get a good night's sleep!

Chapter I

Introduction

Chapter 1 of Understanding Human Behavior is designed to give you a brief introduction to the text. Our goal in this first part of the Student Manual is to familiarize you with several of the exercises which we have suggested in "How to Be a More Successful Student and Still Keep Your Friends." A more comprehensive set of exercises will be found in Chapter 2, which we hope you will incorporate into your study routine.

Let's find out how much you know about human behavior before you read the textbook or take the course. Here is a True/False test made up from the textbook. The answers are given at the bottom of page 27.

1. T F The brain is so delicate that destruction of the connecting band of fibers between the two halves of the cerebral cortex causes loss of coordination and mental confusion.

2. T F During brain surgery you must be deeply anesthetized or you

will experience severe pain.

3. T F Experimental efforts to control behavior using remote-control radio signals sent to electrodes implanted in the brain have been unsuccessful.

4. T F Mild punishment is the fastest and most long-lasting way of eliminating undesirable actions in others.

5. T F The human sense of taste is so highly developed, people are quite accurate in identifying their favorite brands of cigarettes, beer, or whiskey in controlled tests.

6. T F A child who is partially deaf is much better off than a child who is totally deaf.

7. T F Students participating in sensory deprivation experiments typically report many enjoyable experiences and are reluctant to leave the experiment.

8. T F Most sexual inhibition in humans is related to hormone levels.

9. T F People react to stress in basically the same way.

10. T F Blood pressure and other autonomic functions cannot be controlled by a person's conscious mind.

11. T F Investigation has proven that memories recalled during hypnotic regression are highly accurate.

12. T F Couples with genetic defects are usually very thankful for genetic counselling.

13. T F Too much time spent playing retards a child's development.

14. T F The desire to develop as an individual is strong in most college students, but is absent in most adults.

15. T F IQ tests are constructed to be a direct test of a person's "neural efficiency" and are not influenced by cultural or social background.

16. T F Alcohol, taken in moderate amounts, is a stimulant.

17. T F Most sexual offenders are "over-sexed" people who are highly permissive toward all forms of sexual experiences.

CHAPTER OBJECTIVES

These objectives are provided for instructors who wish to clearly specify the information and skills which students should master as they complete Understanding Human Behavior. We have included them in the Student Manual as a means of clearly stating course goals for both instructor and student. We have found that students do well when instructors clearly indicate those questions students should be able to answer as they read the text.

1. What were the psychological problems faced by Edward T.?
2. Compare and contrast the three views of human behavior used by the author to analyze Edward T.'s problem.

Answers to True/False test

1.	F	7.	F	13.	F
2.	F	8.	F	14.	F
3.	F	9.	F	15.	F
4.	F	10.	F	16.	F
5.	F	11.	F	17.	F
6.	F	12.	F		

3. What were the psychological problems faced by Clarence B.?
4. Describe the author's analysis of Clarence B.'s problem.
5. List the author's biases.
6. Describe the advantages to the psychologist of using the scientific method.

ACTION PROJECT 1

How to Be an Empiricist

Which person's statements do people trust the most?:
_____ The person whose ideas are based on opinions and conjecture.
_____ The person who bases his thinking on facts and tested ideas.

The second person, sometimes called an "empiricist," is trusted most. His or her explanation is almost always more accurate than views based on conjecture, speculation, or opinion.

One of the best places to locate facts and tested ideas in psychology is in the library. The fastest way to track down up-to-date information on the topic you want to know about is to start with the Psychological Abstracts. It will be located at a reference desk near the psychology section. The next time you have a chance, go find it and look through it.

What topic would you like facts about? IQ testing of minority children? What causes feelings of friendship? Effects of marijuana on coordination? The role of self-esteem in successful students?

Start by turning to the subject index at the back of the volume. When you find your topic, the number next to it is its abstract number (not page number). Then look back through the volume until you find the number and locate the abstract. It will be a brief summary of the nature of the research and the main findings. If you want to read the entire research report, information is given about how to locate the report in the psychological journal where it was published.

Chapter 2

YES, A CHART! AND THAT'S NOT ALL!

One goal of this manual is to make your course work rewarding and relevant to your needs as a student in psychology. We have described a course of action which, if incorporated into your study routine, will facilitate your efficiency and effectiveness as a student. As you complete each of the steps described in the pages ahead, it will be helpful to record your progress on the chart we have provided on the next page.

Recording a step completed, a test mastered, or a reward earned is a useful way to tally your daily and weekly accomplishments. The chart will also serve as a motivational device encouraging you to follow these steps.

Students do well when they follow the steps we suggest and have listed on the chart. We also know that the chart is a good means by which you can keep score of your success in learning, so go ahead and give it a try. Other students have benefited from it and we expect that you will too.

Your Chart

Steps	Chapters								
	2	3	4	5	6	7	8	9	10
1. Have read questions 1-5									
2. Surveyed the chapter									
3. Generated questions 6-10									
4. Answered questions 1-10 after surveying chapter									
5. Generated a summary									
6. Re-read the chapter quickly									
7. Re-wrote and revised answers to questions									
8. Took true-false test									
9. % correct on T/F test									
10. Generated practice test									
11. Listed rewards									
12. Took practice test									
13. % correct on first practice test									
14. No. of times I took practice test to reach mastery									
15. Level of mastery reached (%)									
16. Reward earned									
17. Exchanged practice test									
18. % of test questions guessed									
19. Reward earned for questions guessed									

Your Chart

Steps	Chapters									
	11	12	13	14	15	16	17	18	19	20
1. Have read questions 1-5										
2. Surveyed the chapter										
3. Generated questions 6-10										
4. Answered questions 1-10 after surveying chapter										
5. Generated a summary										
6. Re-read the chapter quickly										
7. Re-wrote and revised answers to questions										
8. Took true-false test										
9. % correct on T/F test										
10. Generated practice test										
11. Listed rewards										
12. Took practice test										
13. % correct on first practice test										
14. No. of times I took practice test to reach mastery										
15. Level of mastery reached (%)										
16. Reward earned										
17. Exchanged practice test										
18. % of test questions guessed										
19. Reward earned for questions guessed										

Your Chart

Steps	Chapters									
	21	22	23	24	25	26	27	28	29	30
1. Have read questions 1-5										
2. Surveyed the chapter										
3. Generated questions 6-10										
4. Answered questions 1-10 after surveying chapter										
5. Generated a summary										
6. Re-read the chapter quickly										
7. Re-wrote and revised answers to questions										
8. Took true-false test										
9. % correct on T/F test										
10. Generated practice test										
11. Listed rewards										
12. Took practice test										
13. % correct on first practice test										
14. No. of times I took practice test to reach mastery										
15. Level of mastery reached (%)										
16. Reward earned										
17. Exchanged practice test										
18. % of test questions guessed										
19. Reward earned for questions guessed										

Either tear the chart out of this book and post it in a highly
visible place where you study, or keep it in your book. Keep the chart
up to date. This makes it easy to record your accomplishments as soon
as they happen. It is important that you are always aware of your daily
progress. You'll be surprised at the positive effect it will have on
your success!

Quickly look over the chart and then go over the next few pages,
which tell you how to use it effectively.

A HELPFUL HINT!

We hope you have read the introductory section, "How to Be a More
Successful Student and Still Keep Your Friends." It was designed to
teach you methods of succeeding in any course you encounter in your
educational career. If by accident you skipped over that section please
go back and review it. It is the key to mastering Understanding Human
Behavior. If you are familiar with this section, you are prepared to
proceed through the following steps and master the textbook with good
speed and comprehension.

PREDICTING EXAMINATION QUESTIONS

Before reading the chapter please read these questions but don't
answer them yet!

1. What role does the cerebral cortex play in the management of your
    bodily functions?

2. Describe the difference between a petit mal seizure and a grand mal
    seizure.

3. Why is Dilantin prescribed for people who experience epileptic
    seizures?

The answer to every item in the introductory quiz is False.

4. What is the function of the corpus callosum?

5. Why did John Doe's doctors severe his corpus callosum?

Step 1

Now give yourself a check mark on the chart for having completed
Step 1. Next, using the speed-reading techniques we have discussed,
survey Chapter 2 of the text quickly and generate five questions of
your own.

6.

7.

8.

9.

10.

<u>Steps 2 and 3</u>

Give yourself two more checks on your chart--one for surveying Chapter 2 of the text and one for generating five questions.

What next? Now attempt to answer Questions 1-5 and 6-10 based on what you remember from your survey. This is asking a lot from you, but don't worry about how accurate your answers are at this time. Your answers will improve as you continue using this strategy with future chapters. Go ahead now and answer the questions as well as you can.

<u>Step 4</u>

Give yourself a check for attempting to answer Questions 1-10.

Now that you have ten questions and answers it is time to make your first attempt at writing a summary. In generating the summary remember to make it brief, and include:

(a.) The important questions you believe the author was attempting to answer.
(b.) The answers or conclusions the author wants people to reach.

Go ahead and write the best summary you can now, even if you believe you won't do very well. It is necessary to take this step in order to train your mind to automatically grasp the main points in the material you read.

YOUR SUMMARY

<u>Step 5</u>

Give yourself a check on the chart for attempting to generate a summary. Well done! By attempting to answer the questions and write a summary you are using your time wisely.

RE-READ AND RE-WRITE

Use your speed-reading techniques to re-read the chapter as quickly as possible to revise, confirm, or elaborate the answers you wrote after simply surveying the chapter. Then revise the answers to the point where you believe they are as close to 100 percent correct as your instructor would expect.

Step 6

Give yourself a check for re-reading the chapter.

Step 7

Give yourself a check for revising or rewriting your answers to the questions.

LET'S TEST THE TEST

Here is a chance to find out how much you've learned. Take our True/False test. Check to see what percentage you have correct by surveying the chapter.

1. T F It is in your cerebral cortex where decisions are made about what actions to take.
2. T F The three main components of a nerve cell are the dendrite, axon, and soma.
3. T F The synapse is a small fiber connecting the ends of neurons together.
4. T F Delta waves are the small, fast electrical waves generated by your brain when you are deeply asleep.
5. T F The resting potential is the amount of stored-up electrical energy each nerve cell contains.
6. T F Drugs such as Dilantin are given to patients to facilitate the firing of their brains in hypersynchrony.
7. T F The right cerebral hemisphere has dominant control over the right side of your body.
8. T F The corpus callosum acts as a kind of trunk line connecting the two halves of the brain.
9. T F When the corpus callosum is intact, information that reaches one cerebral hemisphere is almost automatically flashed to the other.
10. T F In most split-brain patients one hemisphere usually gains complete control and is able to control both sides of the patient's body.

Step 8

Give yourself a check for taking the True/False test.

Step 9

Please record your percentage of correct answers. _____% correct

GENERATING A PRACTICE TEST

   Generate a test which you believe will be exactly like the one your
instructor will give. Refer back to the section on generating practice
tests if you have any questions.
   Your test could be composed of: True/False
                                    Multiple choice
                                    Fill in
                                    Short answer
                                    Matching
                                    Essay

Step 10

   Give yourself a check for generating a practice test.

THE BIG PAY-OFF

   Just what you've been waiting for--a little remuneration for a lot
of hard work. Set up a list of rewards for yourself for achieving
different levels of mastery on your own test. Here is an example of the
rewards set up by a successful student:

                100% = Movie
                 90% = Three hours of favorite TV shows
                 80% = A large hot fudge sundae
                 70% = A magazine

Step 11

   Give yourself a check for setting up a list of rewards.

TESTING YOURSELF

   Take your test under conditions as similar as possible to those
under which the instructor will test you. Refer to the section on test-
taking if you have any questions.

Step 12

   Give yourself a check for taking your practice test.
   After you have completed the test, check your answers to determine
the percentage of questions you answered correctly the first time you
took the test.   _____ % correct

Step 13

   Record your percentage correct on your first practice test.
   If you did not score 100 percent the first time, feel free to retake
the test until you have demonstrated mastery. You can keep taking the
test until you are able to obtain a perfect score.

Step 14

Record on your chart the number of times you took the test until you attained a perfect score, or the level of mastery you set as your goal.

Step 15

Record the level of mastery you attained.

Step 16

At last! The reward! Go ahead and collect on the reward you earned Record which reward you earned on your graph.

SWAPPING

Arrange with a classmate to swap practice tests. This will help both of you.

Step 17

Tally how many practice tests you exchange with classmates on your chart.

THE LAST FOR BEST--ANOTHER REWARD

Here is the crucial move in the game of saving time, learning a lot, and making studying pleasant. Plan to reward yourself for the percentage of questions on each test or quiz given by your instructor which you have predicted. (Check the study skills section on predicting exam questions.)

List the rewards you will receive for predicting questions on tests or quizzes which are based on Chapter 2 (or Chapter 2 combined with others):

Percent Predicted		Reward
100%	=	
90%	=	
80%	=	
70%	=	

Step 18

After the exam, record on your chart the percentage of questions you were able to anticipate. Calculate your percentage by comparing your list of test questions with the questions on the instructor's exam.

Step 19

Record on the chart the reward you earned for the percentage of questions you guessed correctly.

What's the purpose of all this questioning, testing, and checking of steps completed? The more you do this, the more your mind will begin to follow these steps out of habit. In the meantime the chart gives you daily feedback as to how well you are achieving the goal of becoming a more intelligent person and excellent test-taker. Your options are clear. Good luck!

CHAPTER OBJECTIVES

1. What is the function of the cortex?
2. Draw a model of the physical structure of the brain and label each section.
3. Analyze the possible consequences of damaging input neurons and processing neurons.
4. Describe the three main components of each nerve cell and their interrelated functions.
5. How does epilepsy occur in the brain?
6. How does the neuron pass information from one part of the body to another?
7. How is the EEG used to detect brain damage?
8. Compare and contrast the difference between synchronous brain patterns and hypersynchronous patterns.
9. Describe the chemical causes of epilepsy.
10. Specify the difference between a <u>petit mal</u> seizure and a <u>grand mal</u> seizure.
11. What is the major difference between the right and left cerebral hemispheres?
12. Describe the function of the corpus callosum.
13. What is the role of the major cerebral hemisphere?
14. List the similarities between an epileptic seizure and a positive feedback loop.
15. Discuss the results of the split-brain studies of Myers and Sperry.
16. Describe the most common effects of splitting the human brain.
17. Define the following terms: cerebrum, cortex, neuron, dendrite, soma, cell body, axon, resting potential, synapse, activity pattern, spindles, hypersynchrony, synchrony, corpus callosum, transmitters, sensory pathways, motor pathways, <u>grand mal</u> seizure, <u>petit mal</u> seizure, motor epilepsy, receptor cell, processing cells, motor neurons, EEG, alpha waves, delta waves, cerebral hemispheres, ambidextrous.

ACTION PROJECT 2

Take a Brain-wave Trip

Every one of your movements, feelings, and thoughts is accompanied by neurological activity. This is why psychological research must often be coordinated with neurological research.

At present, one of the best sources of information about neurological activity in humans is the electroencephalograph (EEG). It is quite likely that you and several classmates could visit a nearby EEG lab to learn about how an EEG is done. Arrange for such a visit if you can, because it will give you a better understanding of the material in your textbook; and if you are interested in using biofeedback equipment, you might pick up some practical tips.

The various machines advertised as being able to give you feedback about your brain-wave state are nothing more than simple EEG machines.

OUTSIDE READINGS

Deutsch, Anthony J. "Neural Basis of Memory," _Psychology Today_, vol. 1, no. 12 (May 1968), pp. 56-61

Kamiya, Joe. "Operant Control of EEG Alpha Rhythm and Some of Its Reported Effects on Consciousness," in _Altered States of Consciousness_, Charles Tart, ed. (New York: John Wiley & Sons, Inc., 1972), pp. 519-529.

Walter, Grey W. _The Living Brain_ (New York: W.W. Norton & Company, Inc., 1963).

Chapter 3

IMPORTANT!

In the spirit of efficiency we ask that you use your chart as a checklist for following the steps necessary to master the material in each chapter. By following the same steps for each chapter you will increase the probability of your succeeding in the course. This chapter will serve as a transition. All of the steps are listed, but without explanations or comments. Refer back to Chapter 2 for procedures whenever necessary.

Starting with Chapter 4, each of the remaining chapters will provide you with: the authors' questions and space for your answers, space for your questions and answers, space for your summary, a true/false test, and chapter objectives.

WHAT'S THE PAY-OFF?

By following the steps we have outlined, you will create a manual which contains:

1. 10 questions and answers for each chapter.
2. A summary of each chapter.
3. A true/false test for each chapter.

And you will have a folder which contains

4. All of your practice tests and answers.
5. All of the questions and answers generated from classmates' tests, class notes, and old exams.

The result will be that when it comes time for midterm and final exams, all you will have to do is review your manual and folder. You will have a comprehensive set of questions and answers which, as you gain experience, will be very similar to the exam the instructor gives you.

PREDICTING EXAM QUESTIONS

Before reading the chapter please read these questions but <u>don't answer them yet</u>!

1. What are the four conditions of Nirvana?

2. How does alcohol act as an inhibitor of neural activity?

3. What effect do barbiturates or downers have on the parasympathetic nervous system?

4. According to McConnell, what is a drug?

5. What conclusions did the 1973 Presidential Commission on Marijuana and Drug Abuse reach after extensive research?

<u>Step 1</u>

(Check off the steps here and on your chart as they are completed.)

YOUR QUESTIONS

6.

7.

8.

9.

10.

Steps 2 and 3 _____ and _____

Step 4 _____

YOUR SUMMARY

(Check off these steps here and on your chart as you complete them.)

Step 5 _____

Step 6 _____

Step 7 _____

TESTING THE TEST

1. T F The state of Nirvana is physiologically very different from one person to another.
2. T F The function of inhibitor chemicals is to facilitate synaptic transmission.
3. T F Alcohol is a depressant for most humans.
4. T F Uppers, or stimulants, have their greatest effect on the sympathetic nervous system.
5. T F Activity in the parasympathetic nervous system acts as an inhibitor of activity in your sympathetic nervous system.
6. T F Analgesics act to block out neural messages before they can reach the brain and be perceived as hurting.
7. T F Opiates prevent the pain signal from reaching the brain.
8. T F Hallucinogens have an effect opposite from analgesics.
9. T F THC is almost never fatal when taken in large doses.
10. T F Biofeedback techniques are used to achieve control of alpha rhythm activity.

(Check off Steps 8-19 on your chart as you complete them.)

SPECIAL BONUS!

Most instructors do not give an exam until the first few textbook chapters have been covered. This means that at this time you have probably not yet had a chance to earn rewards in Steps 18 and 19.

If you have been completing these steps we outlined, are working at learning how to ask and answer questions quickly, and have been recording your progress on the chart then you deserve a special treat.

Efforts to acquire new skills and habits are always difficult at first so if you have stayed with it this far you have earned a reward. We suggest going out and treating yourself to a nice big banana split or other goody of your choice.

CHAPTER OBJECTIVES

1. What four types of biological changes typically accompany altered states of consciousness.
2. Describe the function of inhibitor chemicals and give an example as to how they may operate.
3. What is the excitatory-inhibitor process?
4. How does alcohol act as an inhibitor?
5. List the basic characteristics of a drug.
6. How do uppers or stimulants affect the sympathetic nervous system?
7. How do downers or barbiturates affect the parasympathetic nervous system?
8. What is the difference between consciousness and unconsciousness?
9. Describe the function of analgesics.
10. Describe the function of opiates.
11. How do hallucinogens affect the sensory processes?
12. What is the major psychological danger of hallucinogens?
13. Describe the various medical and social uses of cannabis throughout history.
14. What is the effect of cannabis on central nervous processes and short-term memory?

15. List the conclusions of the 1973 Presidential Commission on Marijuana and Drug Abuse.
16. Interpret the relationship between the yoga experience and alteration of brain-wave patterns.
17. Why is it difficult to control your own alpha activity?
18. Define the following terms: altered states of consciousness, receptor sites, inhibitors, excitatory neurons, transmitters, inhibitory neurons, depressant, inhibitory centers, uppers, stimulants, sympathetic nervous system, amphetamines, parasympathetic nervous system, barbiturates, tranquilizers, consciousness, stream of conscious, brain cycle, opiate, morphine, heroin, analgesic hallucinogens, LSD, mescaline, ergot, euphorics, cannabis, THC, time distortion, nicotine, trance state, transcendental meditation, activity rhythm, alpha waves, biological feedback.

ACTION PROJECT 3A

A Time to React

Have you ever looked up from your reading to see your pen rolling off the edge of the desk, but found that you couldn't react fast enough to catch it? The delay between when we see or hear something and when we react to it is called "reaction time."

You have probably noticed that some drivers react to green lights faster than others, that some pedestrians react to the "walk" signal faster, and some sprinters and swimmers react to the starting gun faster than others. Psychologists have found that people vary in their reaction times just as they vary in height, weight, strength of grip, lung capacity, IQ score, and so on.

Reaction time cannot be measured with a stop watch because the reaction time of the person using the stop watch cannot be controlled. This is why special electronic or photographic equipment is often used. There is a way, however, for you to get an accurate measuring of reaction time using a ruler.

Seat your subject at a table. Position him or her so that the elbow, forearm, and the side of the hand are resting on the surface and his or her fingers extend past the edge. Tell the subject to hold his or her thumb and index finger about one inch apart.

Holding one end of a ruler between your own thumb and index finger, dangle it so that the other end is in the space above the subject's fingers. Position it so that the zero line is level with the top of the fingers.

Explain to your subject that when you release the ruler he or she is to catch it between his or her fingers the moment it starts to fall. After it is caught, the distance from the end of the ruler (the zero line) to the point under the middle finger shows exactly how far the ruler fell.

All solid objects fall at the same rate so the reaction time can be calculated to the 1000th of a second. The table below will allow you to convert distance into time without having to do the calculations for each person.

Inches		Seconds
1	=	0.072
2	=	0.102
3	=	0.125
4	=	0.144
5	=	0.161
6	=	0.176
7	=	0.190
8	=	0.203
9	=	0.216
10	=	0.227
11	=	0.238
12	=	0.250

If you are curious about the mathematics, here is the formula for calculating the speed of falling:

$$\underline{d} = \tfrac{1}{2}\ \underline{g}\underline{t}^2$$

$$\underline{t}\ (secs) = \frac{\sqrt{\underline{d}\ (inches)}}{13.9}$$

where $\underline{d}$ = distance
$\underline{g}$ = gravity
$\underline{t}$ = time

If you are curious about the formula and can't figure it out, check with the nearest physics major.

This test gives you a way to examine questions like: Do men have a faster reaction time than women? Is a right-handed person faster with his right hand? Is a trained athlete faster than an intellectual person? Do drugs or alcohol slow a person down?

After getting experience using a ruler you might want to show off your knowledge by performing a "party" trick. Hold a dollar bill with the picture of Washington directly between the person's fingers. Tell him or her to keep the dollar if he or she can catch it when you let it go. Many people have lost money betting that they could catch the bill.

ACTION PROJECT 3B

Where Are You?

Ask some friends to answer the question: "Where are you inside your body?" Question them to find out as much as possible about their thoughts and feelings on this subject.

Next ask them: "Who are you?" Each time they give an answer ask: "In addition to that, who are you?" Continue until they can't think of anything else. If your interview is going well, you can continue with the question: "Why are you?"

This is an excellent self-development experience and can be used as a group exercise.

Compare the answers given by your friends to the answers given by some children.

PROVOCATIVE QUESTIONS AND ISSUES

People in the drug scene are frequently heard to claim that they have the right to live their lives and do with their minds and bodies what they wish, that society has no right to dictate how they should live their lives. The problem is that there are many instances in which people into drugs take away from other people the right to live _their_ lives as _they_ wish. "The Cause of Death" is a true story which happened to a friend of one of the authors. After reading it, talk over some of the issues of freedom of choice the story raises with a few friends.

THE CAUSE OF DEATH

by Al Siebert

Donna drank the last of her apple juice and decided to get some more. She leaned heavily on the table as she got to her feet because her baby was due in about a week. She felt great. At her pre-delivery check-up the day before the doctor said the baby was in the right position and had a strong heart beat.

"Your health is excellent," he told her, "and you should have no trouble with the delivery since this will be your fifth child."

Donna dropped the serving ladle back into the pot and returned to her table. She grew sad for a moment as she glanced around the room and observed her surroundings. Three years ago she was living in a $20,000 home in Vancouver, Washington. Her husband, Jon, was president of a company he started himself and their future looked bright. But Jon was a genius. He couldn't stay put. He needed to explore new frontiers. He sold the business, bought an abandoned hot springs resort in California, and opened it up to anyone who wanted to move in. Donna didn't want to uproot the children but she loved Jon and knew that he had to follow his dreams so she went with him.

This had been a fine resort in its day but now the place was in disrepair. The window next to her bed was broken and glass kept falling out. Her household belongings were still in cardboard boxes scattered around the sunporch.

Sometimes Donna felt trapped. Most of the people who moved in were Hippies. It quickly turned into a Hippie community. She had to ask the group treasurer for money when she wanted to buy clothes for her children. She adapted as well as possible and devoted herself to her children.

Though 34, and accused of being "too straight," Donna was trusted by the young people and many of them came to her for advice. Some were drug "freak-outs" but mostly it was just the ones who couldn't take the pressures.

Drugs were a touchy subject at the resort. Jon would go along with almost anything--even nudity was O.K.--but not drugs. Finally, after persuasion didn't work, Jon declared:

"Either the drugs go or I go."

But today there was no time to worry about drugs or run-down buildings. This was Saturday, February 22nd, 1969, the day of the big fellowship meeting. Donna left the dining room and started searching for several friends she was expecting. She couldn't find them but suddenly she didn't care because she was going numb all over. She recognized the feeling. She knew it was LSD because she had been talked into trying it once.

She saw Jon and grabbed him.

"It's LSD. I've been given LSD. It must be in the food!"

Jon rushed to the kitchen. "What's going on?" he demanded. "Who put LSD in the food?"

No one was sure but the kitchen crew did know that the apple juice had LSD in it, put there by someone who wanted to help the meeting get its "feet off the ground."

Jon put Donna into the car, gathered up the children and headed for a friend's home in Marin County, California. By the time they arrived the six-year-old boy was extremely sick--a condition that was to last four days--and Donna was feeling labor pains.

They drove to nearby St. Helena Hospital and Donna was admitted to the delivery ward. The doctors examined her and discovered that the unborn child's heart beat was slow and faint.

Hours passed. The doctors watched her carefully.

Then early Sunday morning, eight hours after she drank the apple juice, the doctor straightened up, put his stethoscope away and said:

"The baby's heart has stopped beating."

During the next few hours Donna's labor contractions stopped and the effects of the LSD wore off. She left the hospital and went to her private physician. He started her on hormones to get labor going again.

On February 27th, 1969, the baby was born dead in the Marin County General Hospital. The softened bones of the dead fetus lacerated the sides of Donna's uterus and she bled profusely. She wavered between life and death for several hours before she finally pulled through.

First printed in Northwest Magazine (December 14, 1969). Reprinted by permission.

OUTSIDE READINGS

Barber, Theodore, Leo V. Di Cara, Joe Kamiya, Neal E. Miller, David Shapiro, Johann Stoyva, eds. Biofeedback and Self-Control (Chicago, Ill.: Aldine-Atherton, Inc.), 1971.

Cushman, John. The LSD Story (New York: Fawcett World Library), 1966.

Castaneda, Carlos. The Teachings of Don Juan: A Yaqui Way of Knowledge (New York: Ballantine Books, Inc.), 1968.

Nowlis, Helen H., Drugs on the College Campus (Garden City, N.Y.: Anchor Books), 1969.

Chapter 4

PREDICTING EXAM QUESTIONS

1. What was the theory of homunculus?

2. What famous discovery was made by Fritsch and Hitzig during the Franco-Prussian War?

3. What are the three theoretical viewpoints regarding the determinants of violence?

4. What conclusions did Azrin draw from his research on aggression?

5. What is the consequence of removing parts of the limbic system from vicious animals?

YOUR QUESTIONS

6.

7.

8.

9.

10.

YOUR SUMMARY

TESTING THE TEST

1. T F The theory of phrenology stated that there were no connections
          between an individual's personality and his physical charac-
          teristics.
2. T F Boroca discovered that specific areas of the brain control
          specific types of psychological and mental activities.
3. T F Physiological psychologists study how functions of the brain
          affect behavior.

4. T F From an intrapsychic standpoint you determine little of what you think, feel, and do.
5. T F From a social viewpoint, if you want to change your mind, you must first change your environment.
6. T F Lorenz was able to demonstrate that some animals have stereo-typed aggressive reactions.
7. T F Azrin was able to demonstrate that attack behavior in animals is instinctual rather than learned.
8. T F Azrin found that the aggressive syndrome occurred regardless of whether the frustrated animal was given an alternative of escaping rather than attacking.
9. T F According to Dollard and Miller, aggression is always caused by frustration.
10. T F Emotional behavior of higher organisms is, to a great extent, controlled by the limbic system.

PROVOCATIVE QUESTIONS AND ISSUES

1. Do you believe that people who are easily angered by others could control themselves better if they were taught about the causes of aggressive reactions?

CHAPTER OBJECTIVES

1. What is the mind-body problem and why is it of significance to psychologists?
2. Describe the theory of homunculus and its relative usefulness to the field of psychology.
3. List the three assumptions upon which Gall's theory of phrenology is based.
4. What was the purpose of Flouren's neurological experimentation?
5. Describe Broca's neurological research.
6. Name the four main sections or lobes in each cerebral hemisphere.
7. Describe the discovery of the electric probe by Fritsch and Hitzig.
8. Compare and contrast the biological, intrapsychic, and social/ behavioral views of the mind-body problem.
9. What is the significance of Blumenthal's research on attitudes toward violence?
10. Describe Lorenz' research and conclusions on aggressive behavior.
11. Describe the research and conclusions of O'Kelly and Steckle on pain and aggression.
12. What is the significance of Azrin's research on aggression?
13. What is the frustration-aggression hypothesis of Dollard and Miller?
14. List the functions of the limbic system.
15. Describe the research and conclusions of Kluever and Bucy on the limbic system.
16. What is the significance of Delgado's research on radio control of the limbic system?
17. How did Mark and Ervin use the stimoceiver to diagnose brain damage?

18. What is Mark and Ervin's theory regarding neurological causes of violent behavior?
19. Define the following terms: stimoceiver, instinctual behavior, homunculus, phrenology, electric probe, association areas, biological viewpoint, intrapsychic viewpoint, social/behavioral viewpoint, frustration-aggression hypothesis, limbic system, decorticate.

ACTION PROJECT 4

Programmed Aggression

Researchers estimate that by the time the average child has finished high school he or she will have spent 11,000 hours in classrooms and 15,000 hours watching television. Concern is being expressed about the impact television has on children because evidence shows that children tend to imitate behaviors that bring approval or success to others.

Spend a Saturday morning watching a number of children's cartoon shows and commercials to see how much violence there really is. Use the chart on the next page to tally the frequency of violent acts in these shows.

When you are done, evaluate what you have observed. What kinds of examples for action have been presented to boys and girls? What kinds of foods are children urged to eat? What kinds of toys is it suggested they ask for? If a child imitated what appeared on these shows, and did as instructed by the commercials, what would he or she be like? What effect might this have on children's reactions to death and violence in real life?

If your findings move you to want to do something about children's television, send a copy of your report to: Action for Children's Television, 46 Austin Street, Newtonville, Massachusetts, 02160. They welcome information from all parts of the country and will send you information about their organization.

OUTSIDE READINGS

Ardrey, Robert. The Territorial Imperative (New York: Atheneum Publishers, 1966).
Azrin, Nathan. "Pain and Aggression," Psychology Today, vol. 1, no. 1 (May 1967), pp. 26-33.
Bakan, David. "Is Phrenology Foolish?", Psychology Today, vol. 1, no. 12 (May 1968), pp. 44-50.
Murray, John P. "Television and Violence: Implications of the Surgeon General's Research Program," American Psychologist, vol. 28, no. 6 (June 1973), pp. 472-478.

Key: x = action of character caused a death.

√ = act of violence; character hits or shoots someone or causes someone to be struck.

Name of cartoon and running time	Creatures			Human Male		Human Female		Antagonists talked out differences and became friends
	Animal good/bad	Monster good/bad	Robot good/bad	Hero	Villain	Heroine	Villainess	

Chapter 5

PREDICTING EXAM QUESTIONS

1. List some general objectives of intrapsychic therapy.

2. What is the major difference between directive and non-directive therapy?

3. According to behavioral therapists, why do people acquire habitual patterns of behavior?

4. How does one extinguish undesirable behavior?

5. According to Smith and Walter, why is it important for children to have a structured and stable environment?

YOUR QUESTIONS

6.

7.

8.

9.

10.

YOUR SUMMARY

TESTING THE TEST

1. T F Psychoanalytic therapy usually involves having the patient
          develop insight into his behavior.
2. T F Non-directive therapists frequently give patients detailed
          instructions as to what they should think and do.
3. T F When reinforcement for a behavior no longer occurs, the beha-
          vior will extinguish.

4. T F A terminal behavior pattern is usually so complex it cannot be recognized or easily measured.
5. T F Behavioral therapies seldom use rewards or reinforcements.
6. T F According to behavioral therapists, we seldom learn new behaviors because we find them rewarding.
7. T F Smith and Walter do not believe that children function best in environments with defined rules.
8. T F In behavior therapy undesirable behavior is eliminated by using mild punishment.
9. T F In behavior therapy it is important to quickly reward any small changes or improvements in the desired direction.
10. T F Many children who are labeled minimally brain-damaged have simply never learned the types of appropriate behavior evident in other children.

PROVOCATIVE QUESTIONS AND ISSUES

1. Some people argue that using behavior modification to shape the behavior of others is too manipulative. Yet it is clear that regardless of whether or not we intend to shape the behavior of others we are always doing so--in many cases to their detriment. Wouldn't it be better for our society if required courses in behavior modification were taught in all schools? Wouldn't this prevent many of the tragic results which occur now because people are haphazardly and unknowingly using the principles of behavior modification in ways that develop inappropriate and undesirable behavior in others?

2. We often see people who are extremely overweight. Many of them confess that they would give anything to lose weight. The advice typically offered to such persons is to use self-discipline and will power in order to stop eating. But there is growing evidence that many cases of obesity are not the result of a lack of will power or because of physiological problems. It is simply that these people are constantly reinforced for eating in a gluttonous fashion at home, work, and in social situations. Restaurants are pleased when an obese person orders a huge meal. Friends and relatives are amazed and constantly discuss the quantities of food consumed. The attention given to this person by people dining with him reinforce his eating. The question is: "How could you use a system of reinforcement to shape proper diet selection, eating habits, and weight control procedures with friends, spouse, or parents who face this gigantic problem?"

CHAPTER OBJECTIVES

1. List the important goals of intrapsychic therapies.
2. Describe the goals of environmental therapies.
3. Give several examples of the goals of behavioral therapy.
4. Contrast the differences between directive and nondirective therapy.
5. Identify the differences between psychoanalysis and various humanistic therapies.
6. What are the goals of client-centered therapy?
7. How did Patti K. learn a variety of problematic behaviors?

8. What behavioral techniques did Smith and Walter use to change Patti K.'s behavior?
9. Why did Patti K. spend considerable time screaming and soiling her pants?
10. How did Smith and Walter use extinction training with Patti K.?
11. Give several examples of how people unwittingly reinforce inappropriate behaviors.
12. Give several examples of Smith and Walter's use of successive approximations with Patti K.
13. How did Smith and Walter teach Patti K. impulse control?
14. What is the purpose of establishing clear rules for children?
15. How can a parent establish a stable environment for a child?
16. Define the following terms: behavioral therapy, environmental therapy, reinforcement, extinction, extinction training, terminal behavior, punishment, successive approximation, intrapsychic therapy, psychotherapy, directive therapy, nondirective therapy, humanistic therapy.

ACTION PROJECT 5

Learning to Use Reinforcement and Extinction to Achieve Your Goals

We are often bothered by the actions of others and yet there is no observable way of stopping those actions. Research into the principles of reinforcement suggests that in many cases we may unknowingly be reinforcing undesirable actions in others by simply paying attention to them. Thus, it is important to learn to ignore undesirable behavior and pay attention to those desirable behaviors that are the mirror images of the undesirable actions. By encouraging the desirable behaviors, the undesirable actions may be prevented.

For example, your roommate talks consistently about the terrible weather, scarcity of money, the difficulties of going to school, and dozens of other nauseating topics. Granted, life is rough, but there is little you can do about it at the moment. What you really want is that your roommate is pleasant and does not dwell on all the negative aspects of life. Here's how you do it.

Step 1: Your goal will be to increase the number of pleasant things your roommate says and decrease the number of unpleasant remarks.

Step 2: Your method will be that of reinforcing pleasant talk and ignoring irritating talk. Example: When your roommate says things which you think are positive you should pay close attention, maintain eye contact, nod in agreement, smile, comment favorably after each statement, and generally encourage him or her to talk about pleasant topics.

When your roommate says things which you define as negative, you should be inattentive, look away, try to remain expressionless, and--most important--do not say anything if at all possible. To extinguish negative behavior it is important that you not do things which tend to reinforce it. Thus, you must not provide the attentive behavior which usually reinforces this type of verbal output.

Step 3: Recording the behavior of your roommate is important to your project. During certain periods of time each day, record for 15 minutes the number of positive comments your roommate makes and the number of negative comments. These should be graphed each day. This will allow you to see your progress at reinforcing positive comments and extinguishing negative ones.

Extinction: Remember, behavior increases or decreases as a result of the consequence of that behavior. If you wish to extinguish a behavior, you must not allow it to be followed by something which reinforces it. Most people are reinforced for griping because people listen to them. Even if you tell them to stop griping, you will often find that they continue to do so because they receive attention whenever they gripe.

Reinforcement: Getting rid of griping behavior isn't enough. You can't expect a person to give up talking completely. Thus, it is your job to reinforce your roommate every time he or she says something positive. You will speed up the extinction of negative talk when you reinforce talk which is incompatible with the negative; it's hard to frown when you're smiling.

Step 4: Analyzing your performance should occur after several days of working toward your goal. If the graph shows that your roommate's negative comments are decreasing and positive comments are increasing then you are likely to be reinforcing pleasant talk and ignoring negative talk.

Remember: Griping behavior is likely to be resistant to extinction if it has been reinforced on a variable schedule. It is important that you ignore every negative instance and attend closely to what you want to hear.

If the behavior does not decrease after several weeks, it is likely that you are periodically reinforcing it. If there are other people living with you, they must act in ways consistent with your project, otherwise they will delay your success.

Be careful to look for a trend which you will see in the initial stage of your graph. When you begin withholding attention for the griping behavior, it is likely to increase. Do not be alarmed. Continue ignoring negatives and attend to positives. The more you attend to positives, the faster the negatives will drop off.

Students have succeeded in using this project to change such behaviors as: arriving on time for dates, smiling, eating nourishing foods, and keeping quiet during study hours.

OUTSIDE READING

McConnell, James V. "Why Psychoanalysis Must Go," Esquire, vol. 70, no. 4 (October 1968), pp. 176 ff.

Skinner, B.F. Beyond Freedom and Dignity (New York: Alfred A. Knopf, 1971).

Smith, Donald E.P., and Judith M. Smith. Child Management (Ann Arbor, Mich.: Ann Arbor Publishers, 1965).

Stuart, Richard. Slim Chance in a Fat World (Champaign, Ill.: Research Press, 1971).

Chapter 6

PREDICTING EXAM QUESTIONS

1. What are the free nerve endings?

2. How does your skin determine what objects are smooth and which are rough, if the skin can only experience pressure and temperature?

3. What advantage is there to having the somatic cortex closely related to the motor cortex?

4. Why will even the simplest animal right itself if you turn it on its back?

5. What do the semi-circular canals, saccule, and utricle have in common, and in what ways do they differ?

YOUR QUESTIONS

6.

7.

8.

9.

10.

YOUR SUMMARY

TESTING THE TEST

1. T F The touch receptor cells in the hairy regions of your body
         are different from those in the hairless regions.
2. T F The touch receptor cells in the hairless regions of your body
         are called basket cells.
3. T F The only information you get from your skin is about pressure,
         temperature, and sometimes pain.

4. T F The muscles, joints, tendons, and bones in your hand all have sensory receptors in them.
5. T F The lining of the alimentary canal has the same kind of receptors in it that external skin does.
6. T F Cold detector cells fire more vigorously when the object you touch is very cold than when it is slightly colder than your hand.
7. T F The saccule and utricle detect circular motion.
8. T F Semi-circular canals detect rotary motion of your body.
9. T F The inner ear does not detect motion but senses changes in motion.
10. T F When a person is soaking in a hot bath the water seems to cool rapidly because of habituation.

PROVOCATIVE QUESTIONS AND ISSUES

1. What is your reaction to the statement: "Every scrap of knowledge you have about the world around you, including the people you love and hate, comes to you through the sense impressions you gain from the patterns of neural firing from your sense organs"? If you don't agree with this or don't like the idea, then what is your explanation of how you get knowledge about the world around you?
2. If our sense receptors automatically do what they are supposed to, then why is it that when a person becomes blind his or her remaining senses become much sharper?

CHAPTER OBJECTIVES

1. Describe the operation of pressure receptors.
2. How do pressure and temperature receptors provide feedback to the brain?
3. How does your skin detect smoothness and roughness?
4. How are messages of quality, intensity, and location sent from skin receptors to your brain?
5. What is the function of the somatic cortex?
6. How is the somatic cortex closely related to the motor cortex?
7. Describe how your brain can determine the size, shape, and weight of any object.
8. What is the significance of E.G. Boring's research regarding the sensory processes?
9. Describe the righting response in animals.
10. How is linear motion detected in humans?
11. Describe the function of the saccule and utricle.
12. How does your body detect rotary motion?
13. What is the function of the semi-circular canals?
14. Why do people develop motion sickness?
15. What is the function of the inner ear?
16. Define the following terms: pressure detectors, temperature detectors, temperature receptors, pressure receptors, basket cells, free nerve endings, somatic cortex, righting response, Law of Inertia, saccule, utricle, rotary motion, semi-circular canals, motion sickness, centrifugal force, deep receptors, inner ear.

ACTION PROJECT 6

Sensual Research

Are you better than a robot at knowing which way is up? How good
is your sense of balance when you can't see? How long can you stand on
one foot with your eyes shut? Try this test on people of different ages
and time how well they do. Is it easier for a person to jump up and
down on one foot with his or her eyes shut? What accounts for the
difference?

Our skin contains specialized receptors for different senses. The
location of these receptors can be mapped with some careful work and the
cooperation of a friend.

Have your friend lie down with part of his or her back exposed.
Using charcoal, washable ink, or some other non-permanent marking instru-
ment, draw several 1 x 2-inch rectangles on the person's back. Draw a
second set of 1 x 2-inch rectangles on a piece of paper.

Using an open safety pin or a large straight pin methodically touch
the skin inside the two rectangles with each end of the pin. Tell your
subject to say "dull" or "sharp" whenever they feel anything touching
them. Touch the skin lightly with one end of the pin or the other.
Change back and forth at random so that your subject cannot predict
which end you will use. Be careful not to damage the skin. With a
little practice you will learn to press hard enough so that if there is
a receptor at that spot the person will respond correctly.

Each time you find a receptor, mark its location on the paper rec-
tangle. You will probably be surprised to learn how many spots have no
receptors, and that every area of skin has a different distribution.
If your subject is still cooperative, map out the distribution of receptors in another area, such as the inside of the forearm.

Sometimes it's hard to believe something unless you see it yourself.
No matter what psychologists say, it is hard to believe that when you
are relaxing in the bathtub, the water is not getting colder.

To get some facts about the phenomenon of temperature adaptation
borrow a submersible thermometer which will register up to 120°. Fill
the tub and get it to the temperature you like. Measure the temperature
of the water with the thermometer. Then get in the tub and relax for a
while; when the water seems to have cooled off, measure the temperature
again. Stay in the tub for a while adding more hot water to keep the
water as hot as you like it. After this has gone on for some time,
measure the temperature again.

When you report your results, include some discussion about the
role of adaptation in our other life experiences.

OUTSIDE READING

Geldard, Frank. "Body English," Psychology Today, vol. 2, no. 7
    (December 1968), pp. 42-47.

Chapter 7

PREDICTING EXAM QUESTIONS

1. A person's sense of taste is limited to what four basic sensory qualities?

2. What is the function of olfactory rods, and why is the sense of smell discussed in conjunction with the sense of taste?

3. Why are taste and smell essentially monaural senses?

4. Explain why men tend to prefer stereo sets with large speaker systems while women do not prefer them.

5. Why do people who are born deaf have difficulty learning to speak?

YOUR QUESTIONS

6.

7.

8.

9.

10.

YOUR SUMMARY

TESTING THE TEST
1. T F Sour and bitter are acquired tastes.
2. T F Differences in taste sensitivity tend to be a function of the
        chemical composition of a person's saliva.
3. T F The best way to smell a flower would be to chew it.
4. T F Taste sensitivity is seldom influenced by food additives.
5. T F With training, man's sense of smell could equal that of dogs.
6. T F Children born partially deaf usually have fewer psychological
        problems than those born totally deaf.
7. T F Differences in ear structure explain why more men than women
        tend to prefer music with high notes.
8. T F Small animals can often hear higher notes than man because
        they have smaller cochleas.

9. T F The frequency of a musical tone is related to how high or low the tone sounds to your ear.
10. T F The amplitude of a sound is dependent on its frequency.

PROVOCATIVE QUESTIONS AND ISSUES

1. Now that processors of prepared foods have discovered how to enhance the flavor of foods with chemicals such as monosodium glutamate, a question is being raised about whether it is morally correct for such chemicals to be used in foods. The primary purpose of our ability to smell and taste the flavor in food is to aid us in selecting nourishment that our bodies need. What might be the long-range effect of eating foods that our mouths have been tricked into accepting as desirable to eat?
2. Since the size of the cochlea determines the range of frequencies heard, do children hear sounds that adults do not? How could you test this idea?

CHAPTER OBJECTIVES

1. Describe the physiological make-up and operation of the taste receptors.
2. What are the chemical processes that result in the sensation of taste?
3. Name four basic taste qualities.
4. Why do people have different taste sensitivities?
5. What is the effect on taste sensitivity of MSG and the miracle berry?
6. How does saliva affect taste sensitivity?
7. Describe the physiological make-up and function of the olfactory membrane.
8. What conclusions did Le Maitre reach regarding smell thresholds?
9. Give an example of olfactory habituation.
10. Identify the primary difference between the senses of taste and smell.
11. Why are taste and smell monaural, while hearing is stereo?
12. How is stereo music produced?
13. How is quadraphonic music produced?
14. Identify the function of the anvil, hammer, stirrup, eardrum, and oval window.
15. How does the cochlea function?
16. Compare and contrast the two important aspects of sound waves; frequency and amplitude.
17. Why will a sound be high or low?
18. How do we increase or decrease the loudness of a sound?
19. How does the size of the cochlea affect how well one hears the upper and lower ends of the scale?
20. Why do small animals hear higher notes than men do?
21. Why might men prefer high-fidelity music which is louder than that most women prefer?
22. What is the function of auditory feedback in teaching humans to speak?
23. Contrast the difference between bone deafness and nerve deafness.
24. Why do children who are born partially deaf often have more difficulty learning to speak than children born totally deaf?

25. Define the following terms: papillae, miracle fruit, olfaction, olfactory membrane, habituation, adaptation, chemical senses, somatic cortex, audition, outer ear, middle ear, inner ear, anvil, hammer, stirrup, oval window, basilar membrane, frequency, amplitude, cycle, Hertz, cochlea, bone deafness, nerve deafness, taste buds, synaptic canals, hormones, parietal lobe, monaural, quadraphonic, audition.

ACTION PROJECT 7

Brand "X"

Is it true that one brand of beer tastes better than the rest? Many people think so. The advertisers of beers, cigarettes, hard liquors, coffee, and soft drinks typically claim that their brand tastes better than all the others.

The way to get facts about such claims is to conduct some tests. Find a person who has a strong preference for one brand of cola drink, beer, or cigarette.

Let's say it is a brand of beer. To test the person obtain a bottle of his favorite beer and bottles or cans of three other brands. Refrigerate them for at least a day before the test so that they are all the same temperature. It will be necessary to eliminate identifying cues such as the shape of the bottle, so when it is time for testing use paper cups or identical small glasses. When the bottles are opened, code each cup with a letter to keep track of which brand it is.

Keep your subject in a separate room while you make your preparations. When you are ready to start, blindfold him or her and bring the person to where your experimental equipment is laid out. It is necessary to keep the person from spotting the favorite brand by its color. Line up the cups in a row and refer to them as A, B, C, D. Allow the subject to sample each of the four cups as often as he or she wishes before making a choice as to which one is the favorite brand. It is usually best to provide your subject with a glass of water and to seat the subject so that he or she can rinse out his or her mouth.

After the subject has made a guess, rearrange the cups and ask him or her to choose again. Do this four times with each subject. Your record sheet will look something like this:

TASTE TEST   Subject's name:_____
                                              Date:_____
Test #1   Preferred brand:_____
    Sequence A B C D
                                  Subject's choice:_____

Test #2
    Sequence C A D B   Subject's choice:_____

Test #3
    Sequence D C B A   Subject's choice:_____

Test #4
    Sequence B D A C   Subject's choice:_____

OUTSIDE READING

Johnson, Hugh. <u>The World Atlas of Wine</u> (New York: Simon and
    Schuster, Inc., 1971).

Chapter 8

PREDICTING EXAM QUESTIONS

1. What standard has been developed for measuring the intensity of
    light?

2. What are the functions of rods and cones?

3. What does it mean to be nearsighted? What physiological conditions
    cause this?

4. Why are sentries and lookouts trained to look at dimly lit objects
    at night out of the corners of their eyes?

5. What are complementary colors? Give examples.

6.

7.

8.

9.

10.

YOUR SUMMARY

TESTING THE TEST

1. T F The smallest, most elementary unit of light is the argon.
2. T F There is a close correlation between the wave length of a
visual stimulus and the color a person experiences.

3. T F The receptors for color vision are rods.
4. T F As people age they tend to become farsighted.
5. T F Cones are non-functional in dim light.
6. T F Bats only have rods and chickens only have cones in their eyes.
7. T F It is possible to produce all visible colors from mixtures of only three hues.
8. T F Color saturation refers to the strength or richness of a color.
9. T F Most color-weak individuals show a deficiency in their response to blue and yellow hues.
10. T F Farsightedness results in distant objects appearing fuzzy and near objects rather clear.

PROVOCATIVE QUESTIONS AND ISSUES

1. The colors for traffic signals were selected without knowing that red-green color blindness is the most common type of color vision defect. What two steps have been taken by traffic safety engineers to correct for this problem?
2. When you make contact with the telephone company about having a telephone installed you will choose between having a black or a colored telephone. Black is not a color, while all other hues (including white) are colors. In making this distinction the telephone company is scientifically correct. When we see black we are seeing no colors, and when we see white we are seeing a mixture of all colors. What this means is that, contrary to popular opinion, the blacker a person's skin, the less colored he is; and the whiter a person's skin, the more colored he is. What this also means is that the National Association for the Advancement of Colored People may eventually have to change its name.

CHAPTER OBJECTIVES

1. Diagram the makeup of the visible spectrum.
2. How do scientists measure the wave length of light?
3. What is the meaning of light intensity?
4. How would you measure the intensity of light?
5. List the function of the pupil, iris, cornea, and aqueous humor.
6. What is the function of the retina and fovea?
7. Describe the function of the rods and cones in your eyes.
8. Why is human color vision best when one looks at something straight on?
9. How does the brain accommodate for the presence of the blindspot?
10. Give an example of the process of color constancy.
11. How do nearsightedness and farsightedness occur?
12. What is meant by the condition of presbyopia?
13. Why does discrimination of objects depend on cone vision?
14. Give an example of the process of dark adaptation.
15. How does Vitamin A prevent night blindness?
16. Why are sentries trained to look at dimly lit objects out of the corners of their eyes?
17. Why are cones non-functional under dimly lit conditions?
18. Why are bats nocturnal animals?
19. Why would chickens go to bed early?

20. Identify the difference between hue and saturation.
21. Why are some people said to be color weak?
22. Why do some people develop partial color blindness?
23. Identify the cause of total color blindness.
24. Define the following terms: photon, visible spectrum, nanometers, amplitude, ultra-violet, pupil, iris, cornea, vitreous humor, photo-sensitive surface, aqueous humor, hue, retina, rods, cones, optic nerve, color constancy, fovea, blind spot, saturation, rhodopsin, farsighted, nearsighted, nocturnal, old-sightedness, presbyopia, color weak, dark adaptation, night blindness, peripheral nervous system, central nervous system, visual adaptation, Snellen Chart, color blindness, mixture chart, Holmgren wools, albinism.

ACTION PROJECT 8A

Swyndell's Ghost

Most seances include a dramatic demonstration which may seem supernatural. In some cases, however, the phenomenon is a natural human experience and there is nothing super about it. One such phenomenon, Swyndell's ghost, occurs because under certain structured conditions the receptors in our eyes hold an after-image for an unusual length of time.

To see the ghost you need a totally dark room, a friend, and a strong flashlight. When you are all set to go, it will be necessary to allow your eyes to become dark-adapted. This will take at least 20 minutes in total darkness. The next step is to aim the flashlight at your friend's face and flash the light on very briefly. (It would be a good idea to practice this several times before the experiment starts.) You must be fast, so that your eyes do not have time to look at different parts of his or her face. It helps to make yourself focus your eyes at the top of the nose.

For the next several minutes after you flash the light you will see Swyndell's ghost every place you look in the room.

If your friend wants to try this with you, it will take about 20 minutes for his or her eyes to become dark-adapted. If you can manage it in the dark, try surprising your friend by holding up a scary mask in front of your face.

If you saw the film 2001: A Space Odyssey, you may have noticed something unusual about the lighting in the pilot's compartment. It was illuminated with red light. Old war movies sometimes show fighter pilots reading, writing letters, and playing games in rooms with red lighting while waiting for their nightly missions.

Red lights are used in such situations because white light saturates the rods in a person's eyes. After being exposed to white light it takes the rods 20-30 minutes to become dark-adapted. This is why it is so much easier to see your way around a theater after you have been inside for a while.

The cones in your eyes provide you with color vision. Thus, in a room illuminated with red light, your cones allow you to see, while your rods become dark-adapted.

Find out for yourself how this works. Obtain a red light bulb and spend part of an evening using it as your only source of light.

To learn more about colors and color vision try playing a card game; try to write something using felt pens with red ink; and look through a book with colored photographs. When you are ready to test your night vision, be careful not to look at any white lights.

Question: What would be the advantages and disadvantages in using red lights for night lighting inside automobiles?

ACTION PROJECT 8B

Helping the Visually Handicapped

Many people do not have visual perception. They must get their information about the world in other ways. The Library of Congress has established a nation-wide program which provides tape recordings for blind and physically handicapped persons. The program is administered through local libraries. Volunteers make tape recordings of books, and the tapes are sent free to people who cannot read because of a handicap.

If you would like to participate in this program or know of someone who could benefit from it (the program has reached only 5 percent of the people eligible for it), contact your local library or write to: Library of Congress, Division for the Blind and Physically Handicapped, 1291 Taylor Street, N.W., Washington, D.C. 20542.

OUTSIDE READING

Rock, Irvin. "When the World Is Tilt: Distortion, How We Adapt," Psychology Today, vol. 2, no. 2 (July 1968), pp. 24-31.

Chapter 9

PREDICTING EXAM QUESTIONS

1. Why were the Chinese somewhat successful in their efforts to indoctrinate American prisoners during the Korean war?

2. How did the Chinese use the principle of successive approximations to shape the behavior of American prisoners?

3. What were the similarities and what were the differences between Chinese and Russian brainwashing?

4. Describe the nature of Donald Hebb's experiments and the conclusions he reached.

5. What is the function of the reticular system?

YOUR QUESTIONS

6.

7.

8.

9.

10.

TESTING THE TEST

1. T F The method of successive approximations was used on American prisoners by the Chinese during the Korean war.
2. T F The Chinese considered brainwashing to be a kind of psycho-therapy and not in the least way coercive.
3. T F Brainwashing is any persuasive technique that involves more-or-less total isolation.
4. T F In the experiments conducted by D.E. Hebb most of the students were able to remain as subjects for over a week.
5. T F Sensory deprivation was found to be exhilarating and enjoyable by most of Hebb's subjects.
6. T F Most of Hebb's subjects reported hallucinations during sensory deprivation.
7. T F The cerebral cortex can directly suppress neural activity in the reticular activating system.
8. T F Most of Hebb's subjects experienced black periods in which they could not think at all.
9. T F A curious finding is that former mental patients with a his-tory of hallucinating are able to withstand sensory depriva-tion and isolation better than people with strong and stable personalities.
10. T F The reticular system acts as an inhibiting system for the rest of the brain.

PROVOCATIVE QUESTIONS AND ISSUES

1. Now that the various techniques of indoctrination and brainwashing are well understood some people are suggesting that we use these techniques on the inmates in our prisons to shape them into being responsible citizens. It is argued that this would be more humane than the present system based on punishment--and more effective as well. What about this? Would you endorse such a program?
2. In what ways do the initiation procedures of fraternities and social groups and the "teaching" methods of Boy Scouts and religious groups resemble brainwashing?

66

CHAPTER OBJECTIVES

1. What is the derivation of the term brainwashing?
2. How were the Chinese able to change American soldiers during their captivity in the Korean War?
3. Give examples of how the Chinese were able to manipulate group rewards to shape good behavior in the Americans.
4. How did the Chinese use the principle of successive approximation to shape soldiers' behavior?
5. How did Stalin's reign induce confessions in prisoners?
6. Describe how the Chinese perceived brainwashing.
7. Compare and contrast the similarities and the differences between Chinese and Russian brainwashing.
8. Identify the differences between brainwashing and indoctrination.
9. How are the techniques of various social, military, and religious groups similar to indoctrination?
10. What is the difference between indoctrination and re-education?
11. What is the significance of Hebb's research on sensory deprivation?
12. Give examples of the psychological changes which took place in Hebb's subjects.
13. How was the break-away effect discovered?
14. Describe Lilly's research and conclusions on sensory deprivation.
15. How was sensory functioning of the nervous system viewed prior to the research of H.W. Magoun?
16. What is the function of the reticular activating system?
17. Give an example of the consequence of surgically removing the reticular activating system.
18. How does the reticular activating system affect attention and habituation?
19. What is the effect of the cortex on the reticular activating system?
20. Describe the relationship between thinking and the reticular activating system.
21. What are the strengths and limitations of brainwashing and sensory deprivation as tools for changing behavior and attitudes?
22. Identify the human factors that determine the degree to which brainwashing and sensory deprivation change behavior and attitudes.
23. Define the following terms: brainwashing, indoctrination, successive approximations, arousal, straight-line sensory system, reticular activating system.

ACTION PROJECT 9

Is Silence Golden?

Sounds pound at us from all directions. Jet planes roar overhead; motorcycles and sports cars race by; truck engines labor loudly; radios and television sets blare; people yell; doors slam; dogs bark; and rock bands blare at us from stereo sets. Noise pollution is getting greater each year. But what about the opposite extreme? What would happen if we suddenly had complete silence?

Locate a plain, quiet room someplace. Try to spend two hours in the room with nothing to look at or listen to--no fair peeking out the window, taking drugs, playing solitaire, or going to sleep. The purpose is to experience what happens to your conscious mind when it is deprived of sensory stimulation. If you can't find a quiet room, use ear plugs or, better yet, conduct your experiment during the early morning hours from about 2 A.M. to 4 A.M.

After you've done this yourself, try to get several friends to do the same thing so that you can compare experiences.

OUTSIDE READING

Brown, J.A.C. Techniques of Persuasion (Baltimore, Md.: Penguin Books, 1963).

Frank, Jerome D. Persuasion and Healing (New York: Schocken Books, Inc., 1963).

Koestler, Arthur. Darkness at Noon (New York: Bantam Books, Inc., 1966).

Sargant, William. Battle for the Mind (London: Pan Books, 1957).

Chapter 10

PREDICTING EXAM QUESTIONS

1. According to McConnell, your brain was pre-wired at birth. Explain why he arrived at this conclusion.

2. What are several examples of reflexive responses in infants?

3. What is the law of learning described as association?

4. What conclusion was Skeels able to reach regarding the relationship of intelligence and environment?

5. What was the nature of the research done by Spitz, and what conclusions did he reach?

YOUR QUESTIONS

6.

7.

8.

9.

10.

YOUR SUMMARY

TESTING THE TEST

1. T F Many of the neural connections between one part of your brain and another were established before you were born.
2. T F Whenever you learn something it is paralleled by some neurological and electro-chemical changes in your brain.
3. T F One of the least important purposes of your brain is that of predicting consequences of actions.
4. T F The more complex a child's associations become, the more difficult he finds it to predict the consequences of his own behavior.
5. T F Skeels found that the changes brought about in children raised by cottage matrons were short-lived.
6. T F Skeels demonstrated that children's IQ's cannot be increased by putting them in enriched environments.
7. T F Mothers who inconsistently reward their children prepare them well for the realities of life.
8. T F Mothers who demonstrate consistent behavior patterns foster dependency relationships in their children.
9. T F Providing sensory stimulation for an infant is apparently just as important as true feelings of love for the child.
10. T F The research of Spitz showed that infants in institutions develop faster and better than infants in slums and ghettos.

PROVOCATIVE QUESTIONS AND ISSUES

1. Research findings, such as those reported in Chapter 10, led to the establishment of the government's Head Start program. Early hopes for the program were not realized, however, as it became clear that the program was reaching many children when they were too old. A stimulating environment for a 3- or 4-year-old cannot fully make up for earlier deprivation. What are your views on this statement and what do you think might be done to reach deprived children earlier?
2. Based on the information presented to you so far, what are your views on the difference between a "good" mother and a "bad" one?

CHAPTER OBJECTIVES

1. Explain how children are neurologically pre-wired at birth.
2. How do children learn new response patterns?
3. How do children learn to discriminate objects?
4. Compare the actions of nerve cells to those of dominos.
5. Describe how your cortical board develops.
6. What is the anaclitic relationship of mother and child?
7. Give an example of information-processing in humans.
8. Describe how the brain predicts the consequences of one's actions.
9. Describe and give an example of the principle of association.

10. How have scientists produced rats with less intelligent brains?
11. What is the relationship between impoverished environments and learning?
12. What is the significance of H.M. Skeel's research on the improvement of IQ's?
13. According to experimental research, what is the difference between a good mother and a poor mother?
14. Describe the research and conclusions of Spitz on "mother love."
15. What are the effects of sensory deprivation on infants?
16. Which components of "mother love" facilitate learning in children?
17. Define the following terms: reflexive, discrimination, assembly of nerve cells, neural transmitter, domino theory, synaptic switches, association, association cortex, IQ, anaclitic relationship, cortical processing, anaclitic dependency.

ACTION PROJECT 10

Take Action, Use ACTION

One of the less well-known ACTION programs is the Foster Grandparents Program. Low-income persons 60 years or older can supplement their incomes by working with mentally retarded and emotionally disturbed children in correctional institutions, residential facilities, and children's hospitals.

Each foster grandparent is assigned one or two children to be with for a few hours each day. The beneficial effects on both the children and the older persons are heart-warming.

Is there a residential center for retarded or disturbed children in your community? Does the center use foster grandparents? Do you know of low-income elderly persons who would welcome an opportunity to be useful?

A little effort on your part might bring together several lonely people who need each other. Check with your local ACTION agency or write to the Foster Grandparent Program, ACTION Domestic Programs, 806 Connecticut Avenue, Washington, D.C. 20525. If you're in a hurry you can call 800-424-8580 toll free.

OUTSIDE READING

Bijou, Sidney. "The Mentally Retarded Child," Psychology Today, vol. 2, no. 1 (June 1968), pp. 46-51.
Goffman, Eric. Asylums (Garden City, N.Y.: Anchor Books, 1961).

Chapter 11

PREDICTING EXAM QUESTIONS

1. What is the difference between sensation and perception?

2. What is the difference between an hallucination and an illusion?

3. Describe and give an example of size constancy.

4. What is the Mueller-Lyer illusion, and why was it important to test it on persons in "circular" cultures?

5. What is Gestalt psychology, and what has it contributed to the understanding of perception?

YOUR QUESTIONS

6.

7.

8.

9.

10.

YOUR SUMMARY

TESTING THE TEST

1. T F Sensory messages coming from your eyes or from any of your sense receptors are called perceptions.
2. T F Sensations are scanned in the lower brain centers to determine if they are important enough to be sent to the cortex.
3. T F Hallucinations do not occur unless some kind of stimulation is received from the external world.
4. T F Size constancy is an illusion in overweight women that sales clerks in clothing stores must deal with.
5. T F People judge heights better than distances.
6. T F According to Gestalt psychologists, shape constancy is the brain's effort to force percepts into more natural forms.
7. T F People who live in circular cultures have very little susceptibility to the Mueller-Lyer illusion.
8. T F The visual cliff was created by Gibson to test inborn depth perception in infants.
9. T F The more intensely you stare at an object the wider your pupil becomes.

10. T F Linear perspective is the coming-togetherness of parallel
          lines as they approach the horizon.

PROVOCATIVE QUESTIONS AND ISSUES

1. The Hess findings that pupillary response is an indicator of one's
   emotional interests opened a highly controversial issue. Some
   employment managers saw the test developed by Hess as a valuable
   tool they could use to find out if any men applying for "security
   sensitive" positions were homosexual. The employment managers
   explained that homosexuality was not the issue. Their problem
   was that when persons afraid of having their homosexuality
   discovered were in jobs with access to secret or classified
   information there was a high risk of the person being blackmailed
   into disclosing secret information.
        If you had a job where it was your responsibility to hire
   people who could be trusted with secret information would you
   feel justified in using a test such as the one on pupillary reflex
   to screen out potential security risks? What arguments might
   there be against using such a test?
2. How many reasons can you think of as to why a one-eyed person has
   more difficulty driving a car than a person with two eyes?

CHAPTER OBJECTIVES

1. Describe the process of scanning.
2. How are sensory messages transmitted to the cortex?
3. How does the process of recognition operate?
4. List the characteristics of a percept.
5. How are hallucinations and illusions produced in the sensory system?
6. Give an illustration of the principle of size constancy.
7. What are the possible consequences of restoring sight to people who
   have been blind since birth?
8. Give an example of the Mueller-Lyer illusion.
9. How are straightness and circularity affected by their context or
   relationship to other objects?
10. What are the effects on one's perceptual process of growing up in a
    circular culture?
11. Illustrate the phenomena of linear perspective and aerial perspective.
12. Describe the process of convergence.
13. Give an example of a figure-ground relationship.
14. Compare and contrast the principles of proximity, closure, continuity,
    and similarity.
15. How do the Gestalt psychologists explain shape constancy?
16. List the principles of perception that have been discovered by
    Gestalt psychologists.
17. Describe the research of Fantz regarding visual perception of
    children.
18. What is the significance of Gibson's research on the visual cliff?
19. Describe Hess's research and conclusions on pupillary behavior.
20. How does the brain select and modify visual inputs?
21. Define the following terms: sensations, images, perception, scanning,
    recognition, percept, hallucination, illusion, size constancy,
    Mueller-Lyer illusion, circular culture, linear perspective,

figure-ground, proximity, closure, continuity, similarity, aerial perspective, visual cliff, convergence, Gestalt.

ACTION PROJECT 11A

Sizing Up Size Constancy

The principle of size constancy is so powerful we are rarely aware of the extreme differences in the actual sizes of images that hit the retinas in our eyes. A car two blocks away looks the same size as a car nearby. A person 6 feet tall looks 6 feet tall 10 feet away or blocks away. To become more aware of differences in image size, hold a ruler up at arm's length and measure the height of the image of a car several blocks away. Do the same with several people three or four blocks away.

ACTION PROJECT 11B

Pupils Can Learn

Learning occurs when experience leads to a change in behavior. You can change the behavior of the pupils in someone's eyes by using classical conditioning.

Take your subject into a dimly lit room. Wait a few minutes for the subject's eyes to become accustomed to the darkness. After the pupils have enlarged, ring a bell. (Note: Any sharp noise will do, such as hitting a glass with a spoon or the top of a desk with a ruler.) In two to three seconds turn a bright light on or flash a flashlight in his or her eyes. The pupil will immediately decrease in size. Turn off the lights and wait a few minutes for the pupils to adapt. Then repeat the loud noise and the light in the eyes. Continue this until you see the effects of the conditioning. After the pupil has dilated in the dark it will begin to contract as soon as the subject hears the noise, even though no light is turned on. Repeat this with several subjects.

OUTSIDE READING

Gibson, Eleanor, and Richard D. Walk. "The Visual Cliff," Scientific American, vol. 202, no. 4 (April 1960), pp. 67-71.

Chapter 12

PREDICTING EXAM QUESTIONS

1. What does the term "threshold" mean?

2. What is the origin of the word "subliminal"?

3. What is perceptual defense, and how did McGinnies explain its function?

4. What is extrasensory perception?

5. Describe Kennedy's experiments on unconscious whispering, and list the conclusions he reached.

YOUR QUESTIONS

6.

7.

8.

9.

10.

YOUR SUMMARY

TESTING THE TEST

1. T F The visual threshold is that intensity of stimulus which you can see one-half the time and cannot see one-half the time.
2. T F A subliminal stimulus is one that you would be conscious of less than one-half of the time.
3. T F Discrimination without awareness always involves stimuli that are below your perceptual threshold.
4. T F Subliminal advertising proved to be such a powerful way to influence people that laws were passed to prohibit its use.
5. T F The senders and receivers in Kennedy's experiments usually became aware of unconscious whispering.
6. T F Belief in ESP has no influence on whether or not a person is a good sender or receiver.
7. T F Motivation is the key to understanding subliminal perception.
8. T F Subliminal stimuli must be detected by the subcortical parts of the brain before they cause a reaction.
9. T F Thorough research into perceptual thresholds has proven that perceptual defense and perceptual vigilance don't really exist.
10. T F Telekinesis is the power to influence the movement of physical objects through mental concentration alone.

PROVOCATIVE QUESTIONS AND ISSUES

1. Why is it important to examine parapsychology phenomena (ESP, clairvoyance, telekinesis, and so on) against the background of research into subliminal perception?
2. If extrasensory perception eventually proves to be an ability that can be developed by people, what impact would that have on their lives? What would your world be like if everyone had the ability to know everything you think and do? What would you do if everyone knew your secrets and you knew theirs? What would schools be like if students could read the instructors' minds to learn the answers to tests?

CHAPTER OBJECTIVES

1. What is the meaning of threshold?
2. What are the differences between perceptual, sensory, and action thresholds?
3. Describe Vicary's subliminal advertising scheme.
4. How does one measure the frustration-aggression threshold?
5. How would you determine a visual threshold?
6. Give an example of a subliminal stimulus.
7. What is the origin of the word subliminal?
8. How was Vicary's claim to fame refuted?
9. What were the results of Suslowa's experimentation of supraliminal and subliminal perception?
10. Describe the concept of discrimination without awareness, and give several examples.
11. Compare and contrast discrimination without awareness and subliminal perception.
12. How does the process of unconscious censoring operate?
13. What was Freud's analysis of the function of repression?
14. Describe the research and conclusions of Bach and Klein in the area of subliminal perception.
15. Describe McGinnies's research and conclusions in the area of perceptual thresholds.
16. Illustrate the concepts of perceptual vigilance and defense, and give several examples.
17. Describe the phenomena of ESP, clairvoyance, telekinesis, precognition, and mental telepathy.
18. Describe J.G. Miller's research and conclusions on ESP.
19. Describe Kennedy's research and conclusions on unconscious whispering.
20. What factors facilitate or inhibit a subject from being a good sender or receiver in ESP experimentation?
21. How did the British attempt to shape the beer-drinking behavior of television viewers?
22. List the conditions under which subliminal stimuli are most likely to affect one's behavior.
23. Define the following terms: subliminal, threshold, perceptual threshold, action threshold, sensory threshold, supraliminal perception, discrimination without awareness, repression, perceptual vigilance, ESP, clairvoyance, telekinesis, unconscious whispering, limen, two-point threshold, perceptual defense, mental telepathy, precognition, psychokinesis, parapsychology.

ACTION PROJECT 12

ESP Testing

A student nurse waited nervously after class until the other students were gone. Then she walked over to where the psychology instructor was putting his materials away and asked, "May I talk to you about something?"

"Certainly," he answered. "What is it?"

"This sounds silly, but two years ago when I was in high school my girl friend and I were fooling around with a ouija board. We asked it who we would marry and stuff. When I asked ouija the name of the man I would marry it spelled out 'Douglas Smithson.' And when I asked about his occupation, ouija spelled out 'physician.'"

"Yes?"

"I just started nursing school this term and last night we were look- ing through the yearbook at the pictures of the medical students. There is a Douglas Smithson who is a senior medical student. I'm scared! What should I do?"

"You could look him up and tell him about the ouija board."

"No!"

"Seriously, the only advice I can offer is to relax, be curious about how things will turn out, and in the meantime don't turn down dates with other medical students."

Psychology has been slow to devote its attention to parapsychological phenomena, so there is not much information available in psychology literature.

To learn more about extrasensory perception, precognition, and such read some or all of the paperback books listed at the end of this chapter. Anyone interested in psychic abilities should include a book about Edgar Cayce in their reading lists. Also a book written by J.B. Rhine.

Your library will probably have copies of the Journal of Parapsychol- ogy, and The Parapsychology Review. These are periodicals which provide a good overview of current developments. If your school library sub- scribes to The American Psychologist, read "ESP and Credibility in Science" by R.A. McConnell in the May 1969 issue.

If you want to conduct some traditional ESP tests, a set of ESP cards and scoring sheets can be purchased for $1.00 from: Foundation for Research on the Nature of Man, Box 6847, College Station, Durham, North Carolina 27708.

There are ways to test for various ESP abilities using materials easily available to you. Try the following experiments to see how well you can do.

Clairvoyance

Get a deck of playing cards and place one red ace and one black ace up on the table. Shuffle the remaining 50 cards several times. Keeping the cards face down, look at the back of the top card. Try to sense what color it is and place it near the ace of that color. Go through the entire deck this way. Follow your hunches and impressions.

When you have finished, turn the piles over and count how many you got right. By chance alone your score will be at least 25. Repeat this procedure three more times and record your score each time. At the end of four trials, your total score by chance alone will be about 100, and this means you did not show any clairvoyant ability.

A score of 114 could happen by accident only once out of 20 times, and suggests you might have some ability. A score of 119 could happen only once in 100 times, and indicates you probably have some ability. A score of 124 could happen only once in a thousand times. If you got this high or higher, you must be good at finding lost objects.

Disbelievers sometimes score low on these tests. If you are a disbeliever and got a score of 82 or lower, you have just demonstrated your clairvoyance, because, at some level of awareness, you had to know what the right choice was in order to consistently make the wrong one. Negative scores (called "psi-negative") are just as significant as positive scores.

Mental Telepathy

You'll need another person for this one. Have him or her sit at a table with the red ace and the black ace face up. You sit across the table with your chair turned around so that your back is to the other person, who is to shuffle the deck several times and place it face down.

When you are ready to start, your helper picks up the top card and concentrates on the color until you say "red" or "black." He or she then places it face down near the ace of the color you named, and looks at the next card. Once you have started, the helper is not to speak until the test is over.

Run through this four times. One hundred right shows no ability; 114, maybe; 119, probably; 124 or over means you probably know a lot more about people than they realize.

Precognition

On a blank sheet of paper make a list of numbers from 1 to 50. Next to each number write down your prediction of the order the red and black cards will be in after they are shuffled. Shuffle the deck a number of times, being careful not to look at the faces. Place the deck face down.

Start with the top card and turn them over one at a time, scoring your list as you go. Do this test four times and add up your total score. As before, 100 means no significance; 114, maybe; 119, probably; 124 or over--you've got an advantage in the stock market.

Psychokinesis

For this test you need a room with no drafts or currents, a small piece of cardboard, a pin, a juice glass, and a square of paper measuring about 2 inches on each side. Set the juice glass upside down on a table. Stick the pin through the center of the cardboard and place it on the bottom of the juice glass.

Fold the paper in the following way: First imagine that the corners are marked like a compass--north, south, east, and west. Now fold the north and south corners together and crease the center. Unfold the paper. Fold the east and west corners together and crease it well.

When you unfold it this time the paper should have a high point in the center and will balance evenly when you place it on the point of the pin.

Sit back and cover your mouth and nose so that your breathing cannot move the paper. Concentrate and try to make the paper spin around. If it moves, try to stop it and move it the other way.

Psychic Pendulum

Tie a piece of thread about a yard long onto one of your rings. Get a piece of notebook paper and draw a large plus sign in the center. Write "no" at each end of one line and "yes" at each end of the other. Place the paper on the floor and let the ring dangle over the center where the two lines cross. Let the ring stop spinning before you start asking questions.

Concentrate on one question at a time. Run a validity check once in a while by asking questions like: "Is my hair brown?" or, "Am I 26?" Do not try to keep your arm or hand under control. Allow them to move slightly if they want to because your purpose is to permit your psychic sensitivity to take over.

For those students curious about how the different significance levels are determined, here is how it is done:

The significance of the scores is determined by starting with a Z-score for each significance level and calculating the standard error of a binomial distribution.

After deciding that a series of 200 guesses will be made, the calculations are:

Standard Error (SE) = $\sqrt{Npq}$ = $\sqrt{200 \times .5 \times .5}$ = $\sqrt{50}$ = 7.1

where SE = standard error
    N = number of trials
    p = probability of success
    q = probability of failure.

probability	= z score x SE	= deviation →	test scores from 200 guesses
.05	= 1.96 x 7.1 =	13.9 ——→	114/86
.01	= 2.58 x 7.1 =	18.3 ——→	119/81
.001	= 3.3 x 7.1 =	23.4 ——→	124/76

A good source to help you work out the math is a statistics major or a graduate psychology student.

If a different number of guesses are made, then a new SE must be calculated. If you go through the deck once with 50 guesses, for example, you cannot divide the 124 by 4 and declare that a score of 31 is significant at the .001 level. The standard error for a trial of 50 guesses is 3.54, which means that to be significant at the .001 level a score of 37 out of 50 must be obtained.

Definitions

Parapsychology: (para = alongside; next to) a field of inquiry exploring mental phenomena; not easily measured by scientific instruments or explained by current levels of scientific knowledge.

Psi phenomena: (psi = mind; mental) the subject matter of parapsychology, just as "human behavior" is the subject matter of psychology.

ESP, extrasensory perception: to have perceptions which did not result from using the ordinary senses.

Clairvoyance: extrasensory perception of distant objects or events.
Mental telepathy: extrasensory communication with another person.
Precognition: to have knowledge about a future event before it occurs;
    a perception which could not result from logic or rational
    inferences.
Psychokinesis: physical movement of an object caused by mental effort
    unaided by any physical energy or instrumentation.

OUTSIDE READING

    Ostrander, Sheila, and Lynn Schroeder. Psychic Discoveries Behind
        the Iron Curtain (New York: Bantam Books, Inc., 1971).
    Sherman, Harold. How to Make ESP Work for You (Greenwich, Conn.:
        Fawcett Publications, Inc., 1964).
    Steiger, Brad. ESP: Your Sixth Sense (New York: Award Books, 1966).

Chapter 13

PREDICTING EXAM QUESTIONS

1. What is the difference between a primary and a secondary drive?

2. What is the relationship between social class and obesity?

3. As presented in the text, what are some of the reasons why fat
   people may be overweight?

4. How does the feeding center and the satiation center work in a
   coordinated effort?

5. What do the letters TAT stand for, and what was Murray's purpose in creating this test?

YOUR QUESTIONS

6.

7.

8.

9.

10.

YOUR SUMMARY

TESTING THE TEST

1. T F Medical treatment of obesity is very successful.
2. T F Eating, overeating, and undereating are all motivated behaviors.
3. T F The satiation center is located in the hypothalamus.
4. T F The feeding center is located in the hypothalamus.
5. T F The hunger pangs that come from stomach contractions are learned.
6. T F All forms of psychotherapy involve giving up old habits and acquiring new ones.
7. T F Murray assumed that people would project their unconscious needs and drives when taking a story-telling test.
8. T F Evidence suggests that some men purposefully encourage their wives to overeat and become fat.
9. T F The conclusion reached by Stuart and others is that whether or not a person loses weight is largely a matter of will power.
10. T F Schachter, _et al_. found that fat subjects when threatened with painful shock ate less than when no threat was present.

PROVOCATIVE QUESTIONS AND ISSUES

1. Why do many people starve themselves on skimpy diets in order to impress strangers with how slender they are?
2. In some corporations candidates for top-level jobs are required to undergo psychological testing in which projective tests, such as the Thematic Apperception Test, are used. What do you believe are some of the advantages and disadvantages of this practice?

CHAPTER OBJECTIVES

1. What are man's primary needs?
2. Describe the theory of homeostasis.
3. Give several examples of secondary needs and drives.
4. Describe the drive reduction theory of motivation.
5. List the traditional medical treatments for obesity and their relative effectiveness.
6. What is the function of enzymes in the digestive process?
7. What is the function of insulin in the digestive process and in controlling hunger?
8. What role does the hypothalamus play in detecting body sugar?
9. What is the effect of stimulating the hypothalamus electrically?
10. Describe the effect on eating behavior of destroying the hypothalamus.
11. Describe the result of combining insulin injections with electrical stimulation of the hypothalamus.
12. List the function of the hypothalamic satiation center.
13. Describe the effect of electrically stimulating the satiation center.
14. How do the feeding center and the satiation center work in a coordinated effort?
15. How is eating behavior affected by the removal of the feeding and satiation centers?

16. How does the swallow counter operate?
17. Describe Stellar's research and conclusions on eating behavior.
18. Describe Cannon's research and conclusions on eating behavior.
19. How are hunger pangs learned, and how is the rate at which they occur changed?
20. Illustrate how one can break the hunger habit.
21. What are the effects of regular and irregular eating habits on the development of hunger pangs?
22. Why are most diet drugs ineffective?
23. What is the significance of Stunkard's research on stomach contractions?
24. What was Freud's theory of intrapsychic influences on hunger and eating?
25. Describe Brusch's research on overweight people.
26. How effective is individual psychotherapy and group therapy with obese patients?
27. What did Warden devise to measure drive strength?
28. How is Murray's Thematic Apperception Test used to measure drive strength?
29. List the strengths and weaknesses of projective tests in determining psychological drives.
30. How useful is the TAT according to McClelland?
31. What is the significance of the research of Schachter on eating behavior?
32. What effect does social class have on obesity?
33. What is the effect of informational feedback on weight gains of individuals?
34. What conclusions did Stuart reach regarding the effects husbands have on the eating behavior of their wives?
35. List the important behaviors a person should incorporate into his or her behavioral repertoire in a weight-loss project.
36. Define the following terms: drive state, primary drives, secondary drives, enzymes, insulin, hypothalamus, feeding center, satiation center, obesity limit, swallow counter, informational feedback, psycho-sexual stages, oral stage, anal stage, fixated, TAT, projective tests, hunger pangs, need achievement, need affiliation, need power.

ACTION PROJECT 13

Mental X-rays

What is obvious to you may not be so obvious to others. One of the fascinating aspects of testing people with the Thematic Apperception Test* is that everyone tells a different story about the same picture.

Look at the picture on the next page. Tell a brief but imaginative story which answers these questions:

What is happening? Who are the persons involved? What led up to the present situation? What is being thought? What is wanted, and by whom? What will happen? What will the outcome be?

_____

*A projective test in which a person attempts to construct meaningful stories in response to a series of pictures.

After you have written your story, ask some other persons to do the same. You can have them write or dictate the stories to you. Don't try to do any interpreting beyond what common sense indicates. Do you agree that psychologists can learn something useful about a person by giving projective tests? What difficulties might psychologists have in trying to interpret the meanings in the stories?

OUTSIDE READING

    Cooper, Kenneth H. The New Aerobics (New York: Bantam Books, Inc.,
        1970).
    Davis, Adele. Let's Eat Right to Keep Fit (New York: Signet, 1970).
    Stuart, Richard B. Slim Chance in a Fat World (Champaign, Ill.:
        Research Press, 1972).

Chapter 14

PREDICTING EXAM QUESTIONS

1. What discoveries did Masters and Johnson make regarding the female
        orgasm?

2. What do sexual and eating behaviors have in common?

3. How does alcohol affect sexual performance in many humans?

4. What was the famous discovery of Olds and Milner?

5. What are the two distinctly different types of pleasure that people experience?

YOUR QUESTIONS

   6.

   7.

   8.

   9.

   10.

YOUR SUMMARY

TESTING THE TEST

1. T F Freud believed that sex was one of the less important motives in human behavior.
2. T F Talk therapies such as psychoanalysis have been very effective in solving problems of female frigidity.
3. T F Sexual behavior in lower animals is almost entirely controlled by sex hormones.
4. T F Primates have more complex sexual behaviors than lower animals.
5. T F Most sexual inhibition in humans is hormonal rather than learned.
6. T F Alcohol works very effectively as an aphrodisiac.
7. T F Deprivation increases the possibility that pleasure centers can be stimulated by the appropriate consumatory behaviors.
8. T F Olds and Milner discovered that the pleasure centers in humans are located in the genitalia.
9. T F Stimulation of pleasure centers in humans is more effective in arousing pleasant sensations than in animals.
10. T F Sexual behavior in people is influenced more strongly by cultural norms, social class, and learned factors than by biological factors.

PROVOCATIVE QUESTIONS AND ISSUES

1. Now that techniques have been developed for implanting electrodes in the pleasure centers in human brains would it not be humane to implant electrodes in the pleasure centers of dying patients so that their last days of life would be filled with pleasurable sensations rather than painful misery?
2. Do you believe there is any danger in the possibility that the leaders of a controlled society might order electrodes to be implanted in the brains of rebellious persons to gain control over them?

CHAPTER OBJECTIVES

1. What is the significance of Watson's attempt to study sexual behavior?
2. Briefly outline Freud's theories on sex as a motivational force.
3. List some of the key contributions of Kinsey's publication Sexual Behavior of the Human Male.
4. Describe Masters and Johnson's discoveries regarding the female orgasm, frigidity, and other aspects of sexual behavior.
5. Name several functions of hormones, the adrenal glands, androgens, and estrogens on sexual characteristics.
6. What is the difference between primary and secondary sexual characteristics?
7. Specify the effects of injecting expectant mothers with estrogens and androgens.
8. Describe the effects on young males and females of over- and underproduction of estrogen and androgen.
9. What is the effect on sexual response patterns when a prevalence of female or male hormones exists during the fetal period?
10. How do the cyclical sexual patterns of animals operate?

11. Compare and contrast sexual patterns of primates and lower animals.
12. Describe the relative effect of hormones and the brain on the sexual behavior of men.
13. What is the effect of hormone injection on frigidity in females and impotence in males?
14. How do injections of androgens and estrogens affect male and female homosexuals?
15. What is the effect of castration on a man's sexual behavior?
16. State the effect of vasectomy on the sexual behavior of males.
17. What were the findings of Murdock regarding the pre-marital sex and adultery taboos in various societies?
18. Compare the effect of the brain circuits on sexual inhibition and behavior in complex and lower animals.
19. List some of the problems of the praying mantis in achieving sexual satisfaction.
20. How does alcohol affect sexual performance?
21. Describe the effect of disinhibitors on sexual behavior.
22. What is the significance of Olds' and Milner's research on the pleasure centers in the brain?
23. What two distinct types of pleasure were discovered by Olds and Milner?
24. How effective is electrical stimulation of a man's or woman's pleasure centers in changing his or her behavior?
25. Define the following terms: erogenous zones, frigidity, repression, hormones, adrenal glands, androgens, estrogens, primary sex characteristics, secondary sex characteristics, disinhibitors, aphrodisiacs, pleasure centers, castration, vasectomy, impotence.

ACTION PROJECT 14

Love Talk

"Mike can enter a party full of strangers and within ten minutes end up on intimate terms with one of the girls. Within half an hour he has cut her out of the pack and is on his way home with her...Mike has an unconscious command of body language and he uses it expertly."

--Julius Fast in Body Language

A fact of life is that some men are much better than others at finding women who will be intimate with them. Some women attract all the men they want and can take their pick, while other women search in vain for just one man.

The difference between success and failure depends largely on how well each person has mastered the art of love talk using non-verbal communication.

One way to understand a skill is to start by watching experts and novices in action. Place yourself in social situations where you can observe:

Several men that women "go for."
Several women that can attract any men they want.
Several men that women usually reject.
Several women that seldom attract male interest.

In your observations study each person's:

Dress and grooming.
Walk, posture, gestures, body positions, and body movements.
Facial expressions, use of lips and tongue, use of eyes.
Proximity to target person, intrusion into personal space.
Physical contact
Use of voice tone, inflections, emotion communicated.

If you observe well, you should easily see that it isn't <u>what</u> a person says but <u>how</u> they say it that counts. In the language of <u>love</u> actions do speak louder than words.

OUTSIDE READING

Belliveau, Fred and Lin Richter. <u>Understanding Human Sexual Inadequacy</u> (New York: Bantam Books, Inc., 1970).
Fast, Julius. <u>Body Language</u> (New York: M. Evans & Co., Inc., 1970).

Chapter 15

PREDICTING EXAM QUESTIONS

1. What are the major divisions of the autonomic nervous system, and what are their functions?

2. Why do people get red in the face when they become angry?

3. According to Selye, what are the three stages the human body goes through in efforts to deal with excessive physiological stress?

90

4. What research helps explain why more American Southerners than Northerners are likely to be killed by tornadoes they know are coming to their areas?

5. What observable traits are characteristic of "externalizers"?

YOUR QUESTIONS

6.

7.

8.

9.

10.

YOUR SUMMARY

TESTING THE TEST

1. T F The autonomic nervous system controls your emotional reactions.
2. T F People who are most sensitive and concerned about the feelings of others have more well-developed sympathetic nervous systems.
3. T F The parasympathetic system tends to excite or arouse you.
4. T F According to Selye, all people have similar physical reactions to stress.
5. T F Cannon concluded that voodoo death is a result of overstimulation of the sympathetic nervous system.
6. T F Externalizers are people who believe they have little or no control over what happens to them.
7. T F According to the Sim-Baumann hypothesis, Southern women in the United States are more likely to believe in luck that Northern women are.
8. T F Characteristic responses to stressful events appear to be something learned at later stages in life.
9. T F Research shows that more Southerners than Northerners are likely to be killed by tornadoes they know are coming to their areas.
10. T F Army and police training techniques using massive doses of stress and punishment are much less effective than training which emphasizes effective coping with difficulties.

PROVOCATIVE QUESTIONS AND ISSUES

1. How is it possible for anyone to believe that they have an internal "locus of control" when there is so much evidence that our actions, feelings, and thoughts are determined by the social forces, sensory stimuli, and reinforcements around us?

CHAPTER OBJECTIVES

1. How is your body similar to a walled city?
2. What is the function of the autonomic nervous system?
3. List the functions of the sympathetic nervous system.
4. List the function of the parasympathetic nervous system.
5. Compare and contrast the sympathetic nervous system and the parasympathetic nervous system.
6. Describe the function of adrenalin and nor-adrenalin.
7. Why does the sympathetic nervous system need a means of keeping itself aroused?
8. Name three distinct aspects of emotional behavior.

9. Describe the three stages Selye states the human body goes through when it mobilizes to meet excess physiological stress.
10. What did Cannon's research on voodoo death indicate were the primary causes of this form of death?
11. Describe Richter's research and conclusions on the consequences of stress.
12. List the conclusions of Sims and Baumann on human response patterns under stress.
13. Why would more Southerners than Northerners be likely to die in tornadoes?
14. Specify the differences in behavioral patterns of people who are internalizers and externalizers.
15. How are response patterns to stress learned?
16. How could a child learn to have a dominant parasympathetic nervous system?
17. List the behavioral patterns that characterize the externalizer.
18. Define the following terms: autonomic nervous system, parasympathetic nervous system, sympathetic nervous system, adrenalin, nor-adrenalin, limbic system, alarm reaction, stage of resistance, stage of exhaustion, externalizers, internalizers, locus of personal control, authoritarian.

ACTION PROJECT 15

Attitude Survey

This test is similar to the Internal/External test developed by Julian Rotter. From each pair of alternatives below select the one that most closely represents your personal belief:

1. ___Promotions are earned through hard work and persistence.　　___Promotions usually come from having the right people like you.

2. ___How hard I study determines the grades I get.　　___I would get better grades if the teaching in this school were better.

3. ___The increasing divorce rate indicates that fewer people are trying to make their marriages last.　　___Fate determines how long a marriage will last. All you can do is hope your partner will stay with you for life.

4. ___When I want to, I can usually get others to see things my way.　　___It is useless to try to change another person's opinions or attitudes.

5. ___In our society a person's income is determined largely by ability.　　___Finding a good-paying job is a matter of being luckier than the next guy.

6. ___If I handle people right, I can usually influence them.　　___I have very little ability to influence people.

7. ___My grades are a result of my effort; luck has little to do with it.　　___Whether I study or not has little effect on the grades I get.

8. ___People like me can change the course of world events by making ourselves heard.　　___It is wishful thinking to believe that one can influence what happens in society at large.

9. ___I am the master of my fate.   ___When I see an unfortunate person, I sometimes think, "There but for the grace of God go I."

10. ___Getting along with people is a skill that can be learned.   ___Most people are difficult to get along with and it is no use trying to be friendly.

11. ___I am usually a good influence on others.   ___Running around with bad company leads a person into bad ways.

12. ___Peace of mind comes from learning how to adapt to life's stresses.   ___I would be much happier if people weren't so irritating.

To score yourself, add up the number of choices you made on the left side of the page. This is your "Internal" score. College students who took this test during the pre-testing with this book obtained scores ranging from 6 to 12.

OUTSIDE READING

Cannon, Walter B. "Voo Doo Death," Psychosomatic Medicine, vol. 19, no. 3 (March 1957), pp. 182-190.

Richter, Curt P. "On the Phenomenon of Sudden Death in Animals and Man," Psychosomatic Medicine, vol. 19, no. 3 (March 1957), pp. 191-198.

Seligman, Martin E.P. "For Hopelessness: Can We Immunize the Weak?" Psychology Today, vol. 3, no. 1 (May 1969), pp. 43-44.

Chapter 16

PREDICTING EXAM QUESTIONS

1. What is the patellar reflex, and why was Twitmyer interested in it?

2. How did Pavlov discover the conditioned reflex?

3. How are researchers able to create "experimental neurosis"?

4. What physiological responses does a polygraph measure?

5. What are the basic principles underlying desensitization therapy?

YOUR QUESTIONS

  6.

  7.

  8.

  9.

10.

TESTING THE TEST

1. T F The patellar reflex can be used for diagnostic purposes to determine brain damage.
2. T F Salivation is an unlearned response elicited by food.
3. T F Pavlov's experiments proved that the nervous system coordinates digestive responses.
4. T F It is more difficult to unlearn conditioned responses than to learn them.
5. T F Pavlov conducted experiments which convinced him that mental illness is learned.
6. T F The polygraph is an emotion detector, not a lie detector.
7. T F Watson and Rayner demonstrated how phobias could be created in children.
8. T F Counter-conditioning is based on the fact that you can easily give two incompatible responses to the same conditioned stimulus.
9. T F Desensitization therapy seldom changes attitudes.
10. T F Psychoanalysts tend to agree with Wolpe's views as to the causes and cures of phobias.

PROVOCATIVE QUESTIONS AND ISSUES

1. Pavlov's conclusions about conditioned reflexes and other learned behaviors have been dominant in Communist countries for many years. Taking Pavlov's research on experimental neurosis into account, in what ways do Russia's actions in international matters resemble the actions of a laboratory scientist attempting to induce neurosis in an animal? Are Russian actions in international matters really as irrational, untrustworthy, and unpredictable as many people believe?
2. In what ways is the American public showing signs that it is becoming desensitized to pornography in films? If it is true that a desensitization process is taking place, then what might be predicted as the next sensitized level to be desensitized?

CHAPTER OBJECTIVES

1. Describe Twitmeyer's research on the patellar reflex.
2. How did Twitmeyer discovery the conditioned reflex?
3. How are the CS, UCS, CR, and UCR interrelated?
4. Describe Pavlov's analysis of the conditioning processes' effect on neural connections.
5. What is the difference between conditioned responses and unconditioned responses?
6. How can one extinguish conditioned responses?
7. Why must the CS be closely paired with the UCS?
8. How did Pavlov train dogs to be masochistic?
9. Describe how Pavlov trained animals to discriminate between different shapes.
10. What is the process of response generalization?
11. How did Pavlov condition neurotic behavior in animals?
12. Describe Liddell's conditioning of experimental neurosis in animals.
13. Describe Masserman's conditioning of experimental neurosis.
14. What was Mowrer's cure for enuresis and what is the psychological theory upon which it was based?
15. Using Watson's research with Albert as an example, describe how fear can generalize.
16. What are the uses and abuses of the polygraph?
17. Describe the counter-conditioning of Little Albert's phobia.
18. Describe Himle's and Shorkey's use of desensitization to eliminate Anna's fear of cars.
19. How did Kraine desensitize J.M. to the sight of blood.
20. Identify the psychological principles underlying desensitization therapy.
21. List the psychoanalytic arguments against the use of desensitization therapy.
22. What is the psychoanalytic view of the underlying causes of phobias?
23. What are Wolpe's arguments against the psychoanalytic interpretation of phobias?
24. Compare relative success rate of desensitization and psychoanalytic therapies in curing phobias.
25. Define the following terms: patellar reflex, conditioned reflex, CS, UCS, CR, UCR, response generalization, enuresis, polygraph, counter-conditioning, phobia, desensitization, discrimination training, neurotic, hierarchy of fears, extinguished, experimental neurosis.

ACTION PROJECT 16A

Twitmeyer's Twitch

E.B. Twitmeyer was the first psychologist to establish a conditioned reflex. He worked with the patellar reflex (knee jerk). You can easily replicate his discovery.

Seat your subject on a desk with one leg dangling freely. Have the subject hold a large paper or some flat object that prevents him or her from seeing when you are going to hit the patellar tendon (located in the soft area just below the knee cap).

When you are ready to begin, seat yourself so that you can first make the sound that will be the conditioned stimulus (CS) and then strike the patellar tendon. It would be best to ring a small bell with one hand and use the other hand to hit the patellar tendon with a rubber reflex hammer. If these items are not easily available, rattle some coins in a tin can for the conditioned stimulus and use the blunt handle of a heavy table knife to hit the tendon.

Conduct a series of short conditioning sessions until the total number of pairings (CS with UCS) is over 100. Then, when you are ready to demonstrate a conditioned reflex, present the conditioned stimulus and watch what happens.

ACTION PROJECT 16B

Palm-reading as Lie-detecting

Note: If it is against your nature to "put people on," then just read this section and don't attempt to do the project. If you do conduct the project, it is essential that you tell each subject afterward that you have been conducting a psychology experiment. If any difficulties arise, talk to your psychology instructor.

We are all capable of subliminal perception. Weak cues and stimuli we are not consciously aware of receiving can influence our perceptions.

Palm-reading is a situation ripe for subliminal perceptions. By holding a subject's hand in yours and making a series of statements it may be possible to detect when you are "hot" or "cold" by sensing the person's heart rate, muscular tenseness, and sweating. Sitting close to the person allows you to sense the breathing rate as well. All of these physiological reactions are measured by modern day "lie detectors."

Ask a number of persons to let you read their palms. Allow your questions and assertions to be guided by cues from their heart rates, breathing, sweating.

Most persons have concerns about money, physical or mental accomplishments, health, work, family, friends, and being loved. Cover each of these areas and let the person's reactions lead you. In matters of work and love most persons are looking for confirmation of what they desire; or they are afraid they are going to find out what they already know is true.

Sample Openings

"You have an interesting palm. Life line (pause), head line (pause), love line (pause). There's something in your life line here. Have you had a serious illness?"

If the response is "no," ask "Childhood illnesses?" (A good escape from any "no" is: "Someone in your family or close to you?")

"I see concerns about money. Is that true? There are hard times ahead, but good fortune later (pause). If you are very careful about signing contracts...you must be careful or you could lose all."

Look up knowingly. "You are a sensitive person. You give others more love than you receive...You've been hurt by someone. You hide your hurt. I see three major loves in your life."

"You are smarter than people give you credit for...you understand people more than they know..."

When you do not hit the target in one area, drop it and move to another. With a little practice you can do about as well as the charlatans who use this technique with gullible persons.

LEARNING THEORY* by James V. McConnell

I am writing this because I presume He wants me to. Otherwise He would not have left paper and pencil handy for me to use. And I put the word "He" in capitals because it seems the only thing to do. If I am dead and in hell, then this is only proper. However, if I am merely a captive somewhere, then surely a little flattery won't hurt matters.

As I sit here in this small room and think about it, I am impressed most of all by the suddenness of the whole thing. At one moment I was out walking in the woods near my suburban home. The next thing I knew, here I was in a small, featureless room, naked as a jaybird, with only my powers of rationalization to stand between me and insanity. When the "change" was made (whatever the change was), I was not conscious of so much as a momentary flicker between walking in the woods and being here in this room. Whoever is responsible for all of this is to be complimented--either He has developed an instantaneous anesthetic or He has solved the problem of instantaneous transportation of matter. I would prefer to think it the former, for the latter leads to too much anxiety.

Yes, there I was walking through the woods, minding my own business, studiously pretending to enjoy the outing so that I wouldn't mind the exercise too much, when the transition took place. As I recall, I was immersed in the problem of how to teach my class in beginning psychology some of the more abstruse points of Learning Theory when the transition came. How far away and distant life at the University seems at the moment! I must be forgiven if now I am much more concerned about where I am and how to get out of here than about how freshmen can be cajoled into understanding Hull or Tolman.

Problem #1. Where am I? For an answer, I can only describe this room. It is about twenty feet square, some twelve feet high, with no windows, but with what might be a door in the middle of the one wall. Everything is of a uniform gray color, and the walls and ceiling emit a fairly pleasant achromatic light. The walls themselves are of some hard material which might be metal since it feels slightly cool to the touch. The floor is of a softer, rubbery material that yields a little when I walk on it. Also, it has a rather "tingly" feel to it, suggesting that it may be in constant vibration. It is somewhat warmer than the walls, which is all to the good since it appears I must sleep on the floor.

The only furniture in the room consists of what might be a table and what passes for a chair. They are not quite that, but they can be made to serve this purpose. On the table I found the paper and the pencil. No, let me correct myself. What I call paper is a good deal rou rougher and thicker than I am used to, and what I call a pencil is

---

*This article was first copyrighted in 1957 by Quinn Publishing Co., Inc., and was reprinted in The Worm Returns: The Best from the Worm Runner's Digest, edited by James V. McConnell (Englewood Cliffs, N.J.: Prentice-Hall, Inc., 1965). It has been widely reprinted throughout the world and is included here as a special bonus. Copyright c 1957 by James V. McConnell.

nothing more than a thin round stick of graphite which I have sharpened by rubbing one end of it on the table.

And that is the sum of my surroundings. I wish I knew what He has done with my clothes. The suit was an old one, but I am worried about the walking boots. I was very fond of those boots--not because of any sentimental attachment nor because they had done me much good service, but rather because they were quite expensive and I would hate to lose them.

The problem still remains to be answered, however, as to just where in the hell I am--if not in hell itself?

Problem #2 is a knottier one--why am I here? Were I subject to paranoid tendencies, I would doubtless come to the conclusion that my enemies had kidnapped me. Or perhaps that the Russians had taken such an interest in my research that they had spirited me away to some Siberian hideout and would soon appear to demand either cooperation or death. Sadly enough, I am too reality oriented. My research was highly interesting to me, and perhaps to a few other psychologists who like to dabble in esoteric problems of animal learning, but it was scarcely startling enough to warrant such attention as kidnapping.

So I am left as baffled as before. Where am I, and why?

And who is He?

2

I have decided to forego all attempts at keeping this diary according to "days" or "hours." Such units of time have no meaning in my present circumstances, for the light remains constant all the time I am awake. The human organism is not possessed of as neat an internal clock as some of the lower species. Far too many studies have shown that a human being who is isolated from all external stimulation soon loses his sense of time. So I will understand that if He wasn't bright enough to leave me with my wristwatch, He couldn't expect me to keep an accurate record.

Nothing much has happened since I began this narrative, except that I have slept, been fed and watered, and have emptied my bladder and bowels. The food was waiting on the table when I awoke last time. I must say that He has little of the gourmet in Him. Protein balls are not my idea of a feast royal. However, they will serve to keep body and soul toge- ther (presuming, of course, that they are together at the moment). But I must object to my course of liquid refreshment. The meal made me very thirsty, and I was in the process of cursing Him and everybody else when I noticed a small nipple which had appeared in the wall while I was asleep. At first I thought that perhaps Freud was right after all, and that my libido had taken over control of my imagery. Experimentation convinced me, however, that the thing was real, and that it is my present source of water. If one sucks on the thing, it delivers a slightly cool and somewhat sweetish flow of liquid. But really, it's a most undignified procedure. It's bad enough to have to sit around all day in my birthday suit. But for a full professor to have to stand on his tiptoes and suck on an artificial nipple in order to obtain water is asking a little too much. I'd complain to the Management if I only knew to whom to complain!

Following eating and drinking, the call to nature became a little too strong to ignore. Now, I was adequately toilet-trained with indoors plumbing, and the absence of same is most annoying. However, there was nothing much to do but choose a corner of the room and make the best of a none too pleasant situation. (As a side-thought, I wonder if the choosing of a corner was in any way instinctive?) However, the upshot of the whole thing was my learning what is probably the purpose of the vibration of the floor. For the excreted material disappeared through the floor not too many minutes later. The process was a gradual one. Now I will be faced with all kinds of uncomfortable thoughts concerning what might possibly happen to me if I slept too long.

Perhaps this is to be expected, but I find myself becoming a little paranoid after all. In attempting to solve my Problem #2, why I am here, I have begun to wonder if perhaps some of my colleagues at the University are not using me as a subject in some kind of experiment. It would be just like McCleary to dream up some fantastic kind of "human-in-isolation" experiment and use me as a pilot observer. You would think that he'd have asked my permission first. However, perhaps it's important that the subject not know what's happening to him. If so, I have one happy thought to console me. If McCleary is responsible for this, he'll have to take over the teaching of my classes for the time being. And how he hates teaching Learning Theory to freshmen!

You know, this place seems dreadfully quiet to me.

Suddenly I have solved two of my problems. I know both where I am and who He is. And I bless the day that I got interested in the perception of motion.

I should say to begin with that the air in this room seems to have more than the usual concentration of dust particles. This didn't seem particularly noteworthy until I noticed that most of them seemed to pile up along the floor against one wall in particular. For a while I was sure that this was due to the ventilation system--perhaps there was an out-going airduct there where this particular wall was joined to the floor. However, when I went over and put my hand to the floor there, I could feel no breeze whatsoever. Yet even as I held my hand along the dividing line between the wall and the floor, dust motes covered my hand with a thin coating. I tried this same experiment everywhere else in the room to no avail. This was the only spot where the phenomenon occurred along the entire length of this one wall.

But if ventilation was not responsible for the phenomenon, what was? All at once there popped into my mind some calculations I had made back when the rocket boys had first proposed a manned satellite station. Engineers are notoriously naive when it comes to a performance of a human being in most situations, and I remembered that the problem of the perception of the satellite's rotation seemingly had been ignored by the slip-stick crowd. They had planned to rotate the doughnut-shaped satellite in order to substitute centrifugal force for the force of gravity. Thus the outer shell of the doughnut would appear to be "down" to anyone inside the thing. Apparently they had not realized that man is at least as sensitive to angular rotation as he is to variations in the pull of gravity. As I figured the problem, if a man aboard the doughnut moved his head as much as three or four feet outwards from the center of the doughnut, he would have become fairly dizzy! Rather annoying it would have been, too, to have been hit by a wave of nausea every time one sat down in a chair. Also, as I pondered the problem, it became apparent that dust particles and the like would probably show a tendency to move in a direction opposite to the direction of the rotation, and hence pile up against any wall or such that impeded their flight.

Using the behavior of the dust particles as a clue, I then climbed atop the table and leapt off. Sure enough, my head felt like a mule had kicked it by the time I landed on the floor. My hypothesis was confirmed.

So I am aboard a spaceship!

The thought is incredible, but in a strange way comforting. At least now I can postpone worrying about heaven and hell--and somehow I find the idea of being in a spaceship much more to the liking of a confirmed agnostic. I suppose I owe McCleary an apology--I should have known he would never put himself in a position where he would have to teach freshmen all about learning!

And, of course, I now know who "He" is. Or rather, I know who He isn't, which is something else again. Surely, though, I can no longer think of Him as being human. Whether I should be consoled at this or not, I have no way of telling.

I still have no notion of why I am here, however, nor why this alien chose to pick me of all people to pay a visit to His spaceship. What possible use could I be? Surely if He were interested in making contact with the human race, He would have spirited away a politician. After all, that's what politicians are for! Since there has been no effort made to communicate with me, however, I must reluctantly give up any cherished hopes that His purpose is that of making contact with genus homo.

Or perhaps He's a galactic scientist of some kind, a biologist of sorts, out gathering specimens. Now, that's a particularly nasty thought. What if He turned out to be a physiologist, interested in cutting me open eventually to see what makes me tick? Will my innards be smeared over a glass slide for scores of youthful Hims to peer at under a microscope? Brrr! I don't mind giving my life to Science, but I'd rather do it a little at a time.

If you don't mind, I think I'll go do a little repressing for a while.

3

Good God! I should have known it! Destiny will play her little tricks, and all jokes have their cosmic angles. He is a psychologist! Had I given it due consideration, I would have realized that whenever you come across a new species, you worry about behavior first, physiology second. So I have received the ultimate insult--or the ultimate compliment. I don't know which. I have become a specimen for an alien psychologist!

This thought first occurred to me when I awoke after my latest sleep (which was filled, I must admit, with most frightening dreams). It was immediately obvious that something about the room had changed. Almost at once I noticed that one of the walls now had a lever of some kind protruding from it, and to one side of the lever, a small hole in the wall with a container beneath the hole. I wandered over to the lever, inspected it a few moments, then accidentally depressed the thing. At once there came a loud clicking noise, and a protein ball popped out of the hole and fell into the container.

For just a moment a frown crossed my brow. This seemed somehow so strangely familiar. Then, all at once, I burst into wild laughter. The room had been changed into a gigantic Skinner Box! For years I had been studying animal learning by putting white rats in a Skinner Box and following the changes in the rats' behavior. The rats had to learn to press the lever in order to get a pellet of food, which was delivered to them through just such an apparatus as is now affixed to the wall of my

cell. And now, after all of these years, and after all of the learning
studies I had done, to find myself trapped like a rat in a Skinner Box!
Perhaps this was hell after all, I told myself, and the Lord High Execu-
tioner's admonition to "let the punishment fit the crime" was being
followed.

Frankly, this sudden turn of events has left me more than a little
shaken.

4

I seem to be performing according to theory. It didn't take me
long to discover that pressing the lever would give me food some of the
time, while at other times all I got was the click and no protein ball.
It appears that approximately every twelve hours the thing delivers me
a random number of protein balls--the number has varied from five to
fifteen so far. I never know ahead of time how many pellets--I mean
protein balls--the apparatus will deliver, and it spews them out inter-
mittently. Sometimes I have to press the lever a dozen times or so
before it will give me anything, while at other times it gives me one
ball for each press. Since I don't have a watch on me, I am never quite
sure when the twelve hours have passed, so I stomp over to the lever and
press it every few minutes when I think it's getting close to time to be
fed. Just like my rats always did. And since the pellets are small and
I never get enough of them, occasionally I find myself banging away on
the lever with all the compulsion of a stupid animal. But I missed the
feeding time once and almost starved to death (so it seemed) before the
lever delivered food the next time. About the only consolation to my
wounded pride is that at this rate of starvation, I'll lose my bay window
in short order.

At least He doesn't seem to be fattening me up for the kill. Or
maybe He just likes lean meat.

5

I have been promoted. Apparently He in His infinite alien wisdom
has decided that I'm intelligent enough to handle the Skinner-Type
apparatus, so I've been promoted to solving a maze. Can you picture the
irony of the situation? All of the classic Learning Theory methodology
is practically being thrown in my face in mockery. If only I could
communicate with Him! I don't mind being subjected to tests nearly as
much as I mind being under-estimated. Why, I can solve puzzles hundreds
of times more complex than what He's throwing at me. But how can I tell
Him?

6

As it turns out, the maze is much like our standard T-mazes, and is
not too difficult to learn. It's a rather long one, true, with some 23
choice points along the way. I spent the better part of half an hour
wandering through the thing the first time I found myself in it. Sur-
prisingly enough, I didn't realize the first time out what I was in, so
I made no conscious attempt to memorize the correct turns. It wasn't
until I reached the final turn and found food waiting for me that I
recognized what I was expected to do. The next time through the maze
my performance was a good deal better, and I was able to turn in a

perfect performance in not too long a time. However, it does not do my ego any good to realize that my own white rats could have learned the maze a little sooner than I did.

My "home cage," so to speak, still has the Skinner apparatus in it, but the lever delivers food only occasionally now. I still give it a whirl now and again, but since I'm getting a fairly good supply of food at the end of the maze each time, I don't pay the lever much attention.

Now that I am very sure of what is happening to me, quite naturally my thoughts have turned to how I can get out of this situation. Mazes I can solve without too much difficulty, but how to escape apparently is beyond my intellectual capacity. But then, come to think of it, there was precious little chance for my own experimental animals to get out of my clutches. And assuming that I am unable to escape, what then? After He has finished putting me through as many paces as He wishes, where do we go from there? Will He treat me as I treated most of my non-human subjects--that is, will I get tossed into a jar containing chloroform? "Following the experiment, the animals were sacrificed," as we so euphemistically report in the scientific literature. This doesn't appeal to me much, as you can imagine. Or maybe if I seem particularly bright to Him, He may use me for breeding purposes, to establish a colony of His own. Now, that might have possibilities....

Oh, damn Freud anyhow.

7

And damn Him too! I had just gotten the maze well learned when He upped and changed things on me. I stumbled about like a bat in the sunlight for quite some time before I finally got to the goal box. I'm afraid my performance was pretty poor.

8

Well, it wasn't so bad after all. What He did was just to reverse the whole maze so that it was a mirror image of what it used to be. Took me only two trials to discover the solution. Let Him figure that one out if He's so smart!

9

My performance on the maze reversal must have pleased Him, because now He's added a new complication. And again I suppose I could have predicted the next step if I had been thinking along the right direction. I woke up a few hours ago to find myself in a totally different room. There was nothing whatsoever in the room, but opposite me were two doors in the wall--one door a pure white, the other jet black. Between me and the doors was a deep pit, filled with water. I didn't like the looks of the situation, for it occurred to me right away that He had devised a kind of jumping-stand for me. I had to choose which of the doors was open and led to food. The other door would be locked. If I jumped at the wrong door, and found it locked, I'd fall in the water. I needed a bath, that was for sure, but I didn't relish getting it in this fashion.

While I stood there watching, I got the shock of my life. I mean it quite literally. The bastard had thought of everything. When I used to run rats on jumping stands, to overcome their reluctance to jump, I used to shock them. He's following exactly the same pattern. The floor in this room is wired but good. I howled and jumped about and showed all the usual anxiety behavior. It took me less than two seconds to come to my senses and make a flying leap at the white door, however.

You know something? That water is ice-cold!

10

I have now, by my own calculation, solved no fewer than 87 different problems on the jumping stand, and I'm getting sick and tired of it. One time I got angry and just pointed at the correct door--and got shocked for not going ahead and jumping. I shouted bloody murder, cursing Him at the top of my voice, telling Him if He didn't like my performance, He could damn well lump it. All He did, of course, was to increase the shock.

Frankly, I don't know how much longer I can put up with this. It's not that the work is difficult. But rather that it seems so senseless, so useless. If He were giving me half a chance to show my capabilities, I wouldn't mind it. I suppose I've contemplated a thousand different means of escaping, but none of them is worth mentioning. But if I don't get out of here soon, I shall go stark raving mad!

11

For almost an hour after it happened, I sat in this room and just wept. I realize that it is not the style in our culture for a grown man to weep, but there are times when cultural taboos must be forgotten. Again, had I thought much about the sort of experiments He must have had in mind, I most probably could have predicted the next step. Even so, I most likely would have repressed the knowledge.

One of the standard problems which any learning psychologist is interested in is this one--will an animal learn something if you fail to reward him for his performance? There are many theorists, such as Hull and Spence, who believe that reward (or "reinforcement," as they call it) is absolutely necessary for learning to occur. This is mere stuff and nonsense, as anyone with a grain of sense knows, but nonetheless the "reinforcement" theory has been dominant in the field for years now. We fought a hard battle with Spence and Hull, and actually had them with their backs to the wall at one point, when suddenly they came up with the concept of "secondary reinforcement." That is, anything associated with a reward takes on the ability to act as a reward itself. For example, the mere sight of food would become a reward in and of itself-- almost as much a reward, in fact, as is the eating of the food. The sight of food, indeed! But nonetheless, it saved their theories for the moment.

For the past five years now, I have been trying to design an experiment that would show beyond a shadow of a doubt that the sight of a reward was not sufficient for learning to take place. And now look at what has happened to me!

I'm sure that He must lean towards Hull and Spence in His theorizing, for earlier today, when I found myself in the jumping stand room, instead of being rewarded with my usual protein balls when I made the correct jump, I discovered...

I'm sorry, but it is difficult to write about even now. For when I made the correct jump and the door opened and I started towards the food, I found it had been replaced with a photograph. A calendar photograph.

You know the one. Her name, I think, is Monroe.

I sat on the floor for almost an hour weeping afterwards. For five whole years I have been attacking the validity of the secondary reinforcement theory, and now I find myself giving Him evidence that the theory is correct! For I cannot help "learning" which of the doors is the correct one to jump through. I refuse to pick the wrong door all the time and get an icy bath time after time. It just isn't fair! For He will doubtless put it all down to the fact that the mere <u>sight</u> of the photograph is functioning as a reward, and that I am learning the problems merely to be able to see Miss What's-her-name in her bare skin!

Oh, I can just see Him now, sitting somewhere else in this spaceship, gathering in all the data I am giving Him, plotting all kinds of learning curves, chortling to Himself because I am confirming all of His pet theories. I just wish...

Almost an hour has gone by since I wrote the above section. It seems longer than that, but surely it's been only an hour. And I have spent the time deep in thought. For I have discovered a way out of this place, I think. The question is, dare I do it?

I was in the midst of writing that paragraph about His sitting and chortling and confirming His theories, when it suddenly struck me that theories are born of the equipment that one uses. This has probably been true throughout the history of all science, but perhaps most true of all in psychology. If Skinner had never invented his blasted box, if the maze and the jumping stand had not been developed, we probably would have entirely different theories of learning today than we now have. For if nothing else, the type of equipment that one uses drastically reduces the type of behavior that one's subjects can show, and one's theories have to account only for the type of behavior that appears in the laboratories.

It follows from this also that any two cultures that devise the same sort of experimental procedures will come up with almost identical theories.

Keeping all of this in mind, it's not hard for me to believe that He is an iron-clad reinforcement theorist, for He uses all of the various paraphernalia that they use, and uses it in exactly the same way.

My means of escape is therefore obvious. He expects from me confirmation of all His pet theories. Well, He won't get it any more! I know all of His theories backwards and forwards, and this means I know how to give Him results that will tear His theories right smack in half!

I can almost predict the results. What does any learning theorist do with an animal that won't behave properly, that refuses to give the results that are predicted? One gets rid of the beast, quite naturally. For one wishes to use only healthy, normal animals in one's work, and any animal that gives "unusual" results is removed from the study but quickly. After all, if it doesn't perform as expected, it must be sick, abnormal, or aberrant in one way or another....

There is no guarantee, of course, what method He will employ to dispose of my now annoying presence. Will He "sacrifice" me? Or will He just return me to the "permanent colony"? I cannot say. I know only that I will be free from what is now an intolerable situation. The chance must be taken.

Just wait until He looks at His results from now on!

From: Experimenter-in-Chief, Interstellar Labship PSYCH-145
To: Director, Bureau of Science

Thlan, my friend, this will be an informal missive. I will send
the official report along later, but I wanted to give you my subjective
impressions first.

The work with the newly discovered species is, for the moment, at a
standstill. Things went exceedingly well at first. We picked what seemed
to be a normal, healthy animal and smattered it into our standard test
apparatus. I may have told you that this new species seemed quite identical to our usual laboratory animals, so we included a couple of the
"toys" that our home animals seem to be fond of--thin pieces of material
made from woodpulp and a tiny stick of graphite. Imagine our surprise,
and our pleasure, when this new specimen made exactly the same use of
the materials as have all of our home colony specimens. Could it be that
there are certain innate behavior patterns to be found throughout the
universe in the lower species?

Well, I merely pose the question. The answer is of little importance
to a Learning Theorist. Your friend Verpk keeps insisting that the use
of these "toys" may have some deeper meaning to it, and that perhaps we
should investigate further. At his insistence, then, I include with this
informal missive the materials used by our first subject. In my opinion,
Verpk is guilty of gross anthropomorphism, and I wish to have nothing
further to do with the question. However, this behavior did give us hope
that our newly discovered colony would yield subjects whose performances
would be exactly in accordance with standard theory.

And, in truth, this is exactly what seemed to be the case. The
animal solved the Bfian Box problem in short order, yielding as beautiful
data as I have ever seen. We then shifted it to maze, maze-reversal and
jumping stand problems, and the results could not have confirmed our
theories better had we rigged the data. However, when we switched the
animal to secondary reinforcement problems, it seemed to undergo a
strange sort of change. No longer was its performance up to par. In
fact, at times it seemed to go quite berserk. For part of the experiment,
it would perform superbly. But then, just as it seemed to be solving
whatever problem we set it to, its behavior would subtly change into
patterns that obviously could not come from a normal specimen. It got
worse and worse, until its behavior departed radically from that which
our theories predicted. Naturally, we knew then that something had
happened to the animal, for our theories are based upon thousands of
experiments with similar subjects, and hence our theories must be right.
But our theories hold only for normal subjects, and for normal species,
so it soon became apparent to us that we had stumbled upon some abnormal
type of animal.

Upon due consideration, we returned the subject to its home colony.
However, we also voted almost unanimously to request from you permission
to take steps to destroy the complete colony. It is obviously of little
scientific use to us, and stands as a potential danger that we must take
adequate steps against. Since all colonies are under your protection,
we therefore request permission to destroy it in toto.

I must report, by the way, that Verpk's vote was the only one which
was cast against this procedure. He has some silly notion that one
should study behavior as one finds it. Frankly, I cannot understand why

you have seen fit to saddle me with him on this expedition, but perhaps you have your reasons.

Verpk's vote notwithstanding, however, the rest of us are of the considered opinion that this whole new colony must be destroyed, and quickly. For it is obviously diseased or some such--as reference to our theories has proven. And should it by some chance come in contact with our other colonies, and infect our other animals with whatever disease or aberration it has, we would never be able to predict their behavior again. I need not carry the argument further, I think.

May we have your permission to destroy the colony as soon as possible then, so that we may search out yet other colonies and test our theories against other healthy animals? For it is only in this fashion that science progresses!

Respectfully yours,
Iowyy

OUTSIDE READING

Stuart, Richard B. Trick or Treatment (Champaign, Ill.: Research Press, 1970).

Wolpe, Joseph. The Practice of Behavior Therapy (Elmsford, N.Y.: Pergammon Press, Inc., 1969).

Chapter 17

PREDICTING EXAM QUESTIONS

1. What basic laws of learning did Thorndike formulate?

2. What did Koehler's famous experiment with monkeys prove?

3. What did Maier's experiments with rats demonstrate?

4. What are the main ideas present in the system of learning expounded by Skinner?

5. What are some of the essential differences between instrumental and classical conditioning?

YOUR QUESTIONS

6.

7.

8.

9.

10.

YOUR SUMMARY

TESTING THE TEST

1. T F Thorndike believed that the learning process in man and lower animals was the same.
2. T F Koehler believed that animals could never achieve higher levels of thinking such as insight.
3. T F Maier's experiments demonstrated that rats could show evidence of insight.
4. T F Positive reinforcement always increases the probability that an organism will repeat a response.
5. T F Terminal behaviors need not be measurable.
6. T F Pavlov believed that closeness in time was enough to bring about an association between a conditioned stimulus and an unconditioned stimulus.
7. T F Programed learning gives the learner continuous feedback as to the accuracy of a response.
8. T F Students taught in classes based on the principles outlined by Skinner tend to learn better than students in traditional classrooms.
9. T F Patients can be taught to control blood pressure through the use of biofeedback equipment.
10. T F According to B.F. Skinner, students don't usually fail to learn, but teachers often fail to teach.

PROVOCATIVE QUESTIONS AND ISSUES

1. There were some major problems with the first guided missiles. They were very expensive especially for something that could only be used once. They needed so much guidance equipment to keep them on target that there was little room left for explosives; and the systems were vulnerable to jamming and disruption by the enemy. During the early part of World War II Professor B.F. Skinner developed a guidance system for missiles that was small, light-weight, low cost, highly reliable, and jam proof. Yet when Skinner's guidance system was presented for consideration to committees of top scientists and military officers it was quickly rejected. Why? They couldn't live with the idea of having U.S. missiles guided by pigeons in steering harnesses.

    How about you? What do you think about the idea and the ethics of using animals for such purposes?
2. It has been suggested that students have the ability to influence an instructor's actions by using operant conditioning techniques. Why might students be reluctant to do this?

CHAPTER OBJECTIVES

1. Describe the research of Thorndike which led to the generation of the learning curve.

2. How was the theory of trial-and-error learning developed?
3. How were the Law of Effect and the Law of Exercise derived; give several examples.
4. What significant effect did Thorndike's research have on American education?
5. Describe the results of Koehler's research with Sultan the Chimp.
6. How did Koehler derive his theory of insightful learning?
7. Describe the research of Tolman which led to his theory of the cognitive map and spatial relationships.
8. Describe Maier's experimentation with Bismark and the development of insightful behavior.
9. List the major differences in the teaching strategies of educators who followed the research of Thorndike and Tolman.
10. List the points of agreement and disagreement between the theories of Pavlov and Thorndike.
11. How was the principle of contiguity developed?
12. How would you teach a pigeon to bowl using the learning theories espoused by Pavlov, Tolman, and Thorndike?
13. Why must you specify entering behaviors, successive approximations, and terminal behaviors when you wish to shape behavior?
14. List the important characteristics of positive reinforcement.
15. How would you teach a pigeon to bowl using the theory of learning espoused by Skinner?
16. How does one chain behavioral responses?
17. Identify the distinctive characteristics of Skinner's theory of learning.
18. What is the effect on behavior of using fixed-ratio schedules of reinforcement?
19. List the functions of the cumulative record.
20. What is the effect on behavior of using a variable-ratio schedule of reinforcement?
21. Identify the principles which underlie the theory of programed instruction.
22. Discuss the practical applications of Skinner's learning theory in classrooms.
23. List some of the basic goals of a behavioral change agent.
24. Why is it difficult for many teachers to incorporate Skinner's principles of learning in their classrooms?
25. What are some of the traditional arguments against Skinner's theory of learning?
26. List some of the basic difficulties in writing programed materials and how these problems can be solved.
27. Specify several differences between classical and operant learning theory.
28. What is the significance of Miller's and DiCara's research into operant control of autonomic responses?
29. Define the following terms: learning curve, trial-and-error learning, Law of Effect, Law of Exercise, insightful learning, cognitive map, spatial relationships, contiguity, terminal behavior, entering behavior, successive approximations, positive reinforcement, chaining, fixed-ratio schedule, variable-ratio schedule, cumulative record, programed instruction, behavioral change agent, operant conditioning, fading, respondent conditioning, biofeedback.

ACTION PROJECT 17

Training a Cat to Come to You*

Cats are independent creatures. They typically come to you only when they feel like it. It is possible to use the principles of operant conditioning to train a cat to come to you when you call it. The first step is to establish a conditioned response to a stimulus under your control using classical conditioning. You will need a neutral stimulus which can acquire reinforcing properties. Choose a sound you can make quickly and easily. A metal "cricket" is excellent, but a squeaky ball-point pen will also work. Snapping your fingers loudly is a possibility. Be careful not to pick a sound which the cat hears all the time, or its conditioned reactions will be extinguished when you aren't around.

Once you have selected the sound you wish to establish as a positive reinforcer, wait until the cat comes around for its meal. Conditioning is established by presenting the neutral stimulus immediately before presenting the unconditioned stimulus. Let's say you've decided to snap your fingers twice. This means that you snap your fingers twice and then immediately set the dish of food in front of the cat. Continue this at every meal and every time you give the cat some special treats.

After about a week you can switch to operant conditioning. When the cat comes toward you, snap your fingers twice. Then, when it arrives, pet it gently or give it a treat. Your aim is to reinforce the behavior of coming to you. Do not snap your fingers or call the cat if it is moving away or hiding. This will weaken the control over the desired behavior.

After about a week you will be ready to test your work. Wait until the cat is relaxed or lightly asleep. Get a delicious treat ready and then snap your fingers twice. The cat will get up and come to you--a bit bewildered perhaps, but it will come.

This same procedure can be used with dogs, birds, or any other animal. It is the basis of what some animal trainers call "affection training."

OUTSIDE READING

Skinner, B.F. "Pigeons in a Pelican," American Psychologist (1960), pp. 28-37.

----------. The Technology of Teaching (New York: Appleton-Century-Crofts, 1968).

Smith, Judith M., and Donald E.P. Smith. Classroom Management (New York: Learning Research Associates, 1969).

Whaley, Donald, and Richard Malott. Elementary Principles of Behavior (New York: Appleton-Century-Crofts, 1971).

---

*Suggested by "How to Teach Animals" by B.F. Skinner, Scientific American, December 1951, pp. 26-29.

Chapter 18

PREDICTING EXAM QUESTIONS

1. What is the difference between Short-term Memory and Long-term Memory?

2. In what way is the Long-term Memory system like the card index system used by libraries?

3. What are mnemonics?

4. According to some scientists, what might RNA have to do with memory?

5. What kind of memory transfer experiments were conducted with planaria?

YOUR QUESTIONS

6.

7.

8.

9.

10.

YOUR SUMMARY

TESTING THE TEST

1. T F To answer any question, you must make use of your memory.
2. T F The Short-term Memory system holds the meaning of incoming
         messages for no longer than several days.
3. T F Most people tend to remember things, rather than recalling a
         few high points and reconstructing the experience.
4. T F A person's Long-term Memory is organized much like the library
         index card system.
5. T F You don't really forget--rather, new learning interferes with
         your ability to retrieve old items.
6. T F The physical representation of memory is called an engram.

7. T F Some scientists believe that memory may be stored in genetic molecules.
8. T F Experiments by Cameron indicate that increased RNA helps older persons avoid senility.
9. T F Without a consolidation period of at least 24 hours the engrams for Long-term Memory will not form.
10. T F In the early memory transfer research with planaria it was found that memory was stored in the tails as well as in the heads of the animals.

PROVOCATIVE QUESTIONS AND ISSUES

1. If by using advanced microbiological techniques the RNA memory engrams from educated and skilled persons could be duplicated for injection into your brain, would you want such an injection. If so, would you want to receive the same engram mixture injected into others?

    Would it be a great step forward for society if, instead of requiring children to go to school, the government required all children to take "memory engram" injections? Would this be one way of insuring an equal education for children of all races in all parts of the country?

CHAPTER OBJECTIVES

1. Describe the sensory information storage stage of information processing.
2. What is the role of the reticular system in sensory-information processing?
3. Give an example of how your short-term memory is thought to operate.
4. Give an example of how your long-term memory is thought to operate.
5. Why are some experiences stored in long-term memory while others are not?
6. How does a person retrieve information that has been stored in a permanent memory bank?
7. List several reasons why forgetting occurs.
8. How would one use mnemonics to improve his or her memory?
9. Why is your brain superior to a computer in its ability to store information?
10. What is thought to be the function of an engram?
11. How have scientists used computer logic to explain the operation of the brain?
12. Describe the effect DNA molecules are thought to have in memory storage and transfer.
13. What were the results of Hyden's research on RNA and memory?
14. What is the effect on memory of injecting chemicals into the brain which destroy RNA?
15. What effect is ribonuclease thought to have on memory?
16. Describe the effect of injecting animals with strychnine during the consolidation period.
17. Discuss the effect of marijuana on short- and long-term memory.
18. What is the effect on the retention of a classically conditioned response when the body of a planarian is severed in half?
19. Describe the effect of injections of ribonuclease on the retention

of a classically conditioned response in a planarian which has regenerated after being split in half.
20. How would you condition a response in a planarian?
21. List the significant results of McConnell's memory transfer experimentation with cannibalistic flatworms.
22. How did McConnell demonstrate the validity of his memory transfer experimentation?
23. How was the reliability of the transfer effect determined?
24. Describe Ungar's work with scotophobin and its effect on the behavior of animals.
25. Define the following terms: long-term memory, sensory information storage, reticular system, short-term memory, mnemonics, engram, DNA, RNA, ribonuclease, strychnine, validity, reliability, computer logic, senility, consolidation, scotophobin.

ACTION PROJECT 18

How to Improve Your Memory

Names

Would you like to have a better memory for people's names? If you are serious about this and are willing to put some effort into improving your memory for names then follow these basic steps:
Create motivation and desire in yourself. Talk to yourself until you are sincerely convinced that remembering names is important for you and important for others.
Decide that you are going to remember names better.
Use the principles of learning that lead to good recall. When you meet someone, immediately say the name out loud. Attach as many associations to the person's name as possible. Ask questions that draw out a picture of the personality and repeat the name frequently during your conversation. Question them about the name ("Hello Jane Jones, do people ever call you J.J.?")

Facts

Special techniques and methods used to improve memory are called mnemonic devices. The first devices were developed centuries ago when the accumulated knowledge of a culture was passed from generation to generation by words of mouth. All of the following can be useful:

Rhymes

It is easier to remember words arranged in rhythmical and rhyming patterns. Many of our best accounts of ancient history are preserved in ballads and lyric poems. Most school children are helped by the rhymes that start "I before e except after c" and "thirty days hath September..." Whenever material proves especially difficult to remember, constructing a rhyme out of it will help. Long-term Memory of the phone number of a friend, for example, might be a rhyme like: "If I want Larry to talk to me dial 957-6413."

Numbering

People in India and the Orient rely heavily on numbers as memory aids. They typically organize information in terms of "the 5 steps to...," "the 7 principles of...," "the 6 levels of...," and so on. Knowing how many items of information are to be remembered helps in recalling them all. When students are asked to name all of the states they know that a complete list must have 50 items.

Acronyms

Sometimes knowing that there are 6 or 8 of something is not enough. More information is needed. One way is to make up a word which contains the first letter of all the items to be remembered. For example, the names and correct sequence of colors in the color spectrum can be recalled more easily by remembering that the first letters spell the name ROY G. BIV (Red, Orange, Yellow, Green, Blue, Indigo, Violet).

If an acronym is too long or too difficult to remember, then a special device called an acrostic can be used. A poem or rhyme is constructed so that the first letter of the words contain the letters of the acronym. If you were trying to memorize the names and numbers of the twelve cranial nerves, for example, the letters OOOTTAFAGVAH can be correctly listed by memorizing the rhyme: "On Old Olympus' Towering Top A Finn And German Viewed A Hop."

OUTSIDE READING

Cohen, Ruth, Wayne King, Glenn Knudsvig, Geraldine Ponte Markel, David Patten, John Shtogren, Rowena May Wilhelm. Quest: Academic Skills Program (New York: Harcourt Brace Jovanovich, Inc., 1973).

Weinland, James D. How to Improve Your Memory (New York: Barnes and Noble, 1970).

Chapter 19

PREDICTING EXAM QUESTIONS

1. How is the "causality fantasy" helpful to charlatans?

2. What is a "placebo"?

3. What explanation did Anton Mesmer have for his "cures"?

4. What therapeutic technique did Freud derive from his experience using hypnosis?

5. Give several explanations of what hypnosis is.

YOUR QUESTIONS

   6.

   7.

   8.

   9.

10.

YOUR SUMMARY

TESTING THE TEST

1. T F Many snake oil remedies contain alcohol.
2. T F A physician who gives a placebo to a patient is a charlatan.
3. T F The investigation of hypnosis was held back because of the bad reputation acquired by mesmerism.
4. T F Freud's investigation of hypnosis marked a turning point in his career.
5. T F According to Hilgard, hypnosis may be a kind of role-playing.
6. T F We perform under hypnosis only those acts we would perform normally in certain situations with the right motivation.
7. T F Investigation has proven that memories recalled during hypnotic age regression are highly accurate.
8. T F Overstimulation of the fast fibers in the spinal cord can inhibit pain.
9. T F According to Melzack and Wall, it is the relative amount of neural activity at the point of the "spinal gate" that controls the sensation of pain.
10. T F Acupuncture appears to decrease the firing of the fast fibers and the cortex's operation of the "spinal gate."

PROVOCATIVE QUESTIONS AND ISSUES

1. When people are accused of being charlatans because they use deceptive means to "cure" others, the justification offered is usually that since people have been helped the method doesn't matter. It is using the idea that "the end justifies the means." The question is, what's wrong with allowing someone to use showmanship and placebos if there are people who benefit?

2. When you read in the textbook the assertion that you would perform anti-social acts if you thought you could get away with them

without being caught, what was your reaction? Were you offended? Did you disagree? If so, let's test this idea with an imaginary situation. Imagine that in a few days you are going to become totally invisible for a period of time. Think for a while about all the things you would like to do while invisible. Are any of the things you would like to do "anti-social"?

3. If hypnosis is role-playing then why couldn't patients in mental hospitals be hypnotized into permanently role-playing what a mentally healthy person is like?

CHAPTER OBJECTIVES

1. Why has the field of medicine always attracted quacks?
2. How does the causality fantasy operate?
3. How may a doctor give a patient a placebo?
4. What was Mesmer's and Paracelsus's view toward mental illness and its cure?
5. Elaborate on Mesmer's cure by hypnotism and the phenomena of the grand crisis.
6. Why was Mesmer banned from Paris?
7. What effect did studying hypnosis have on Freud's theory and practice?
8. Characterize the type of people Hull and others found to be the best hypnotic subjects.
9. What important conclusion did Hilgard reach as a result of his research in the area of hypnosis?
10. Do subjects perform acts under hypnosis which they normally could not? Give several examples.
11. Why did Freud abandon the technique of hypnosis?
12. Describe the theory of hypnotic age regression and the evidence for its validity.
13. What conclusion did Orne reach as a result of his research on hypnotic age regression?
14. List differences between slow and fast fibers.
15. How can physicians detect damage to patients' fast or slow fibers?
16. What is the consequence of stimulating the fast fibers of a patient who is suffering a significant amount of pain?
17. Elaborate on the function of Melzack's and Wall's hypothesized spinal gate.
18. What is the effect on pain of fast fibers firing at a very high rate?
19. What is Melzack's and Wall's analysis of Joseph B.'s lack of pain?
20. What is thought to be the effect of acupuncture on fast fibers in the spinal gate?
21. How was acupuncture discovered?
22. How can a needle inserted between your thumb and forefinger inhibit the pain of a toothache?
23. Discuss the reasons why acupuncture works best with hysteria-like problems.
24. How could acupuncture aid in curing ailments related to the autonomic nervous system?
25. Define the following terms: causality fantasy, placebo, hypnotic regression, slow fibers, fast fibers, spinal gate, acupuncture, hysteria-like problems, Mesmerism, suggestibility, free association, hypnosis, autonomic arousal.

ACTION PROJECT 19A

Self-hypnosis, or How to Entrance Yourself

The dentist straightened up. He looked at the young woman in the chair and said, "You're going to need a filling in that tooth on the right side." As he reached for a hypodermic he asked, "Are you allergic to any anesthetics?"

The young woman shuddered. She hated needles. Hated them so much that she had been practicing self-hypnosis to prepare for this. "I won't need a shot," she announced, enjoying the look of surprise that crossed the dentist's face. "Go right ahead and fill the cavity."

"All right," he agreed skeptically, "but if you change your mind while I'm drilling, I'll give you a shot right away."

She hardly heard his words because she was already slipping into a state of deep relaxation and, in her mind, entering the special, wonderful place where she would pass the time until the dentist finished his work.

All hypnosis is self-hypnosis. Hypnotism is not something done to you; it is something you allow to happen. With practice you can hypnotize yourself. The characteristics of a hypnotic trance are:
     Very deep relaxation
     Heightened awareness of inner self and decreased
          responsiveness to external sensations
     Heightened state of suggestibility

Project

Here is a test you can try if you want to find out if you can put yourself into a trance where you will not experience pain. Put several ice cubes in a dish, then get a towel and find a place where you can sit or lie down and relax without being disturbed. It is important to be comfortable, so loosen any tight clothing. Place the dish with the ice cubes near one hand so that they can easily be reached. Arrange the towel so that when you are holding an ice cube in your hand the dripping water won't bother you or get anything wet.

When you are ready for the test, your hand will reach out and pick up an object from the dish. Do not consciously move your arm. You are merely an observer of your body. When you are ready, your arm will move itself. The object in the dish will seem like nothing more than a child's toy block that is wet. You will be able to hold this block with no discomfort until it melts away and disappears.

There is no danger in putting yourself into a trance because you will be able to bring yourself out of it whenever you choose. Should you fall asleep, you will wake up normally.

If you want to acquire the ability to do self-hypnosis, but cannot, then do some reading on the subject. We recommend Better Health through Self-hypnosis by Leslie M. LeCron (Delacorte Press, 1967).

You might benefit from several sessions with a professionally trained hypnotist. The yellow pages in your telephone directory list psychologists and physicians who specialize in clinical hypnosis. Or you can write to the professional societies for names of practitioners in your area.

You've probably read and heard enough about hypnosis to know what to say and do to induce a trance. Start with your eyes open. Instruct yourself to relax. Focus your attention on relaxing your feet, legs, hands, arms, neck, and so on. Then, as your muscles relax, your eyelids will also relax until they close by themselves.

Note that you should not instruct yourself to go to sleep or get drowsy. Your aim is a very deep relaxation while remaining fully awake. Instruct yourself to ignore distracting noises. Concentrate fully on the relaxation of all your muscles. Take a deep breath once in a while and let it out naturally. Your breathing will slow down and become regular as you drift into a trance.

As your body relaxes and your attention is on yourself rather than on your surroundings, it helps to picture yourself on an escalator which is carrying you down to even deeper levels of relaxation.

For additional information send a stamped, self-addressed envelope to: Society for Clinical and Experimental Hypnosis, 353 West 57th Street, New York, New York 10019; or The American Society for Clinical Hypnosis, 800 Washington Avenue, S.E., Minneapolis, Minnesota 55414.

People have used self-hypnosis to stop smoking, lose weight, control headaches, improve memory, and improve athletic performance. It is a fascinating phenomenon and one which we are a long way from fully understanding.

ACTION PROJECT 19B

Alpha. What's It All About?

As word got around about the experiences people were having during Joe Kamiya's alpha brainwave biofeedback research he started getting so many volunteer subjects it was not necessary to pay them any longer; as the list of volunteers grew, people began offering to pay to be alpha feedback subjects.

There are now dozens of alpha brainwave monitoring devices available from commercial organizations. If you can rent one for a while (we don't recommend that you purchase one until you know what you are doing, because they are expensive), or borrow one from a friend, try it out to see for yourself what states of mind and feelings of relaxation are associated with the alpha condition.

If you can't locate an alpha feedback device, or don't care to rent one, there are several exercises you can conduct which will give you some indication of what a person experiences in the alpha condition.

Focused Attention

Seat yourself in a quiet, comfortable place where there will be few distractions. Place a small object in front of you--such as a pencil, cup, candle, rock, or flower. Focus your attention on the object. Try to avoid thinking about it or talking to yourself. The first few times you try this you will probably be distracted within a few seconds by sounds nearby or thoughts that pull your attention away from the object. With practice, however, you will improve at being able to achieve a higher level of quiet, controlled awareness.

A Silent Trip

Another inner space trip is to sit comfortably in a semi-dark room with your eyes shut while you concentrate your attention on visual images that appear. It is something like learning how to dream while still awake. To succeed at this it is important to learn how to keep your mind silent.

Your Special Place

Many people report that they achieve the alpha condition by imagining themselves relaxing in a very private, special place. This might be on the shore of a lake where the sun is shining, birds are singing, a breeze is blowing, and so on. The more senses one involves, the better it is. Try to feel the gentle warmth of the sun soaking into your body, a soft breeze caressing your face and hair. Take a deep breath to smell and enjoy the clean fresh air that carries a scent of wildflowers. Try to visualize what your special place looks like, feels like, smells like. The more vividly you can imagine and feel yourself in this special place, the faster you will be able to get there. The deep, peaceful relaxation you experience while doing this will give you some understanding of what alpha is all about.

OUTSIDE READING

Barber, Theodore. "Who Believes in Hypnosis," Psychology Today, vol. 4, no. 2 (July 1970), pp. 20ff.

Moss, G. Scott. Hypnosis in Perspective (New York: The Macmillan Company, 1965).

Chapter 20

PREDICTING EXAM QUESTIONS

1. What are DNA and RNA?

2. Why are XXY and XYY chromosomal conditions of concern to psychologists?

3. What is the difference between identical and fraternal twins?

4. What do studies with identical twins show about the effect of practice on early motor development?

5. What is the critical-period hypothesis?

YOUR QUESTIONS

6.

       ———

7.

8.

9.

10.

TESTING THE TEST

1. T F DNA is a nucleic acid found chiefly in the nucleus of a cell.
2. T F The sex of a child is determined by the type of chromosome present in the sperm that fertilizes the egg.
3. T F Sometimes a sperm will have more than one X or Y chromosome in it.
4. T F The endoderm of an embryo will eventually give rise to the muscles, bones, and blood of a child.
5. T F The only way a sperm cell can survive is to mate with an egg cell.
6. T F Fraternal twins are produced by two eggs which are fertilized by the same sperm.
7. T F Much of the human nervous system is not fully developed until the child is a year or two old.
8. T F Studies with identical twins suggest that practice is necessary for early motor development.
9. T F Kagan found that children retarded by social isolation as infants were able to catch up with older children in social and mental abilities by the ages of ten or eleven.
10. T F Most couples with genetic defects have been very thankful for the genetic counseling they received.

PROVOCATIVE QUESTIONS AND ISSUES

1. Since white males with an XYY chromosomal pattern have a much higher than average chance of having a problem with impulse control, do you believe the courts should not hold them personally responsible for acts of violence? Would you be in favor of allowing them to plead "Not guilty by reason of genetic abnormality"?
2. Can you imagine a circumstance in which you would authorize an "embryo transplant" with your unborn child? If you are female can you imagine any circumstance in which you would accept an embryo implant from another woman knowing that the baby was not yours and that you would have to give it up after delivery?

CHAPTER OBJECTIVES

1. What were the behavioral problems of Clyde C., an XYY male?
2. Describe the chemical make-up and function of chromosomes.
3. What is the function of DNA and RNA?
4. How is the sex of a child determined by the combination of chromosomes in its egg and sperm?
5. Why does the condition trisomy-21 or mongolism occur?
6. What is the cause of Klinefelter's Syndrome?
7. Discuss the difference between the XYY male and the XY male.
8. How are identical twins formed?
9. How are fraternal twins formed?
10. Compare and contrast the roles played by the ectoderm, endoderm, and mesoderm in the development of the embryo and fetus.
11. Describe the function of the placenta.
12. Discuss the effect of exercise and practice on a child's motor development, specific skills, and attitude toward physical activities.
13. Describe the critical-period hypothesis of child development.
14. How did Lorenz develop his theory of imprinting?
15. List the data which support and refute the critical-period hypothesis.
16. Illustrate situations in which infants learn to imitate rather than imprint responses.
17. Describe Kagan's research on the effect of early deprivation on childhood development.
18. What must be done to increase the probability that a mongoloid child will learn to read and write?
19. List the advantages and disadvantages of genetic counseling.
20. Define the following terms: XYY condition, chromosomes, DNA, RNA, trisomy-21, mongolism, Kleinfelter Syndrome, XY male, XYY, identical twins, fraternal twins, ectoderm, endoderm, mesoderm, embryo, fetus, placenta, critical-period hypothesis, imprinting, genetic counseling.

ACTION PROJECT 20

Genetic Counseling

After a defective child has been born into a family the parents typically wonder, "Should we have more children? Do we have defective genes?"

These questions are serious and realistic because in some cases a hereditary defect is present in the genes of one of the parents. Fortunately for many such parents and young people worried about hereditary factors a number of genetic counseling centers have been created.

It would be worth your time to visit a genetic counseling center to find out how much is known about genetic factors in human reproduction and what genetic counseling involves.

For information about the location of the genetic counseling center nearest you consult the March of Dimes International Directory for a list of genetic centers; contact the Genetics Department at your nearest university hospital; or write to National Genetics Foundation, 250 West 57th Street, New York, New York 10019.

OUTSIDE READING

Davis, Adele. _Let's Have Healthy Children_ (New York: Signet, 1972).
Ewy, Donna, and Rodger Ewy. _Preparation for Childbirth: A Lamaze Guide_ (Boulder, Col.: Pruett Publishing Company, 1970).
Ingelman-Sundberg, Axel. _A Child Is Born_ (New York: Dell Publishing Company, Inc., 1969).
Hess, Eckard H. "Imprinting in Animals," in _Scientific American_, vol. 198, no. 3 (March 1958), pp. 81ff.
Lorenz, Konrad. _King Solomon's Ring_ (New York: Thomas Y. Crowell and Company, 1952).

Chapter 21

PREDICTING EXAM QUESTIONS

1. How strong is the "maternal instinct"?

2. According to Harlow, what are the five types of social love?

3. The feelings of "love" that an infant monkey experiences toward its mother are determined by what two stimuli?

4. What impact does maternal deprivation have on an infant?

5. To what extent do mothers and fathers in the U.S. inflict physical harm on their children?

YOUR QUESTIONS

6.

7.

8.

9.

10.

YOUR SUMMARY

TESTING THE TEST

1. T F According to Harlow, peer-love grows out of infant-mother love.
2. T F Infant monkeys prefer a cloth mother without a nipple for milk to a wire surrogate mother with milk.
3. T F Infant monkeys become alienated by mothers that ignore or reject them and by mothers that treat them badly.
4. T F The love that an infant monkey has for its mother is determined mainly by warmth and food. The need for contact comfort only emerges after the infant feels secure.
5. T F Monkeys raised on cloth surrogate mothers showed normal adult sexual behavior while those raised on wire mothers did not.
6. T F Taking a baby monkey away from its mother or surrogate mother appears to slow down the baby's maturational process.
7. T F When monkeys raised in isolation were playfully attacked by normal monkeys they would not defend themselves and were almost torn to pieces.
8. T F The maternal instinct in humans is weaker than it is in monkeys.
9. T F When children are raised in a home without a father the personality development of the boys will be affected but not the personality development of the girls.
10. T F Harlow's work suggests that loving is a learned behavior rather than an innate capacity.

PROVOCATIVE QUESTIONS AND ISSUES

1. Harlow's research shows that "unless a female monkey is chased by her age-mates when she is young, she will very likely remain chaste all the rest of her life." Does this imply that we would have fewer lonely spinsters and bachelors in our society if we humans allowed our children to play at adult sexual activity instead of restricting sex education to books, talk, and pictures?
2. What can we learn from the Harlow research that suggests ways in which we can reduce the high level of physical abuse human parents direct toward their children?

CHAPTER OBJECTIVES

1. Describe in objective and measurable terms the phenomena of love.
2. List the evidence against maternal and paternal instincts.
3. Give examples of the five types of social love defined by Harlow.
4. What are the major objections to Harlow's research and to what extent have they been proven valid?
5. How do Harlow's surrogate monkeys differ from live monkeys?
6. Describe the experimentation which led the Harlows to the theory of contact comfort.
7. Which behavioral characteristic of surrogate mothers do young monkeys find most appealing?
8. What evidence led Harlow to state that the basic quality of an infant's love for its mother is trust?

9. Describe the behaviors of monkeys which were trained to be monster monkeys.
10. List Harlow's conclusions regarding the development of an infant's love for its mother.
11. Describe the types of social and sexual behavior the Harlows witnessed when surrogate-trained monkeys were placed together.
12. What are the effects of maternal and peer deprivation on monkeys?
13. How did Shorkey and Taylor counter the effects of maternal deprivation in their hospitalized patient?
14. What is the effect of solitary confinement on monkeys?
15. What behaviors would you expect of female isolate mothers toward their offspring?
16. Identify the factors which may be correlated with child abuse in humans.
17. Compare and contrast the similarities in childhood experiences of humans and monkeys who are abusive parents.
18. What inappropriate behavioral patterns often develop in fatherless males?
19. What inappropriate behavioral patterns often develop in fatherless females?
20. How are the behavioral patterns of fatherless girls affected by their mothers' child-rearing patterns?
21. What is the importance of the child-care experience of siblings as described by Jane van Lawick-Goodall?
22. Why does Harlow's work suggest that loving behavior is learned?
23. How did the Harlows shape isolate monkeys into normal monkeys?
24. Define the following terms: maternal instinct, paternal instinct, surrogate, contact comfort, monster mothers, love, anaclitic depression.

ACTION PROJECT 21

Abused Children

Kevin's father slammed down his newspaper and charged across the room.
"I've warned you about staying away from those matches!" he shouted at his two-year-old son.
He grabbed the back of Kevin's shirt and hauled the boy into the kitchen.
"I'm going to teach you a lesson about staying away from matches," the enraged father declared as he turned on the gas burners on the stove. Then picking up his son by the arms he held the boy's hands in the flames.
"There! You want to see what fire is like? This is what it feels like! No more playing with matches! Do you understand?"
It wasn't until he heard his wife scream behind him that Kevin's father became aware of his son's cries and the smell of burning flesh.

Kevin is one of about 60,000 children subjected to parental assaults and attacks each year. These infants and toddlers are whipped, beaten, choked, smothered, starved, burned, caged, and drugged by their parents. Many children do not survive. Estimates are that about 6,000 children are killed by their parents each year.
Pioneering work into ways of dealing with this problem has been

completed and a need now exists for the public to start demanding corrective programs.

Suggested starting points for action:

Conduct a planned series of observations in shopping centers, supermarkets, and amusement centers. Record the number of instances in which parents hit, pinch, yank, spank, and threaten their children. What is the "normal" amount of physical child abuse in our society?

Call or see the pediatrics units in local hospitals to find out what programs the hospitals have to train physicians and nurses to look for the "battered-child syndrome." Do some research to find out what the "battered-child syndrome" is. Try to find out if your state has laws which allow authorities to take action when the battered-child syndrome has been diagnosed.

Find out if your community has a Parents Anonymous or Families Anonymous group for parents who have abused their children. If no group exists, information about this organization can be obtained by writing to: Families Anonymous, C/O Dr. C. Henry Kempe, Pediatrics Department, University of Colorado School of Medicine, Denver, Colorado, or Mrs. Gertrude Bacon, Executive Director, Parents Anonymous, 250 West 57th Street, New York, New York 10019.

OUTSIDE READING

DeCourcy, Peter, and Judith DeCourcy. A Silent Tragedy: Child Abuse in the Community (Port Washington, N.Y.: Alfred, 1973).
La Leche League. The Womanly Art of Breastfeeding (Franklin Park, Ill.: La Leche League International, 1958).

Chapter 22

PREDICTING EXAM QUESTIONS

1. According to Piaget, what are the two basic processes in human development?

2. Name and briefly describe Piaget's four major stages of intellectual development.

3. What are the basic criticisms of Piaget's theories of development?

4. According to Harlow, what are three types of pre-social play?

5. Name and briefly describe the stages of psychosexual development formulated by Freud.

YOUR QUESTIONS

6.

7.

8.

9.

10.

TESTING THE TEST

1. T F Freud and Piaget would agree that a child's intellectual
           growth passes through several distinct stages or periods.
2. T F Freud and Piaget strongly emphasize the profound influence
           that the environment can have on mental maturation.
3. T F Piaget believes that a child must assimilate facts from the
           world around it, but need not accommodate to the facts.
4. T F The first of Piaget's four stages is the pre-operational stage.
5. T F According to Piaget, the last stage of intellectual develop-
           ment, the stage of formal operations, should be attained by
           the age of 12.
6. T F Child's play seems to be so essential to a child's development
           that the word <u>play</u> doesn't quite fit.
7. T F Freud named the first stage of human development the libidinal
           stage.
8. T F Freud believed that every boy has feelings during the phallic
           stage of desiring his mother sexually and wanting to get rid
           of his father.
9. T F Freud's belief that all human children go through latency is
           not supported by anthropological studies of a wide variety of
           cultures.
10. T F At present there is no one theory that adequately explains
           the function of play.

PROVOCATIVE QUESTIONS AND ISSUES

1. Since child's play seems to have many more purposes than most adults
     realize, should adults take the activity of playing more seriously
     and do more of it themselves?

CHAPTER OBJECTIVES

1. Describe Piaget's theories of assimilation and accommodation.
2. What is the basis of the theory "ontogeny recapitulates phylogeny"?
3. List Piaget's four stages of intellectual development and the beha-
     vioral characteristics which develop during each of them.
4. Discuss the stages of child development postulated by Bruner.

5. How valid are the criticisms of Piaget's theory of child development?
6. Describe the child-rearing patterns of the Nyansongo of Africa.
7. Name the three types of pre-social play hypothesized by Harlow.
8. List the three types of social play.
9. What is the function of rough-and-tumble play hypothesized by Harlow?
10. How does Piaget view creative play?
11. What is the significance of Hall's research on doll play?
12. How did Levin and Wardell use doll play as a projective technique?
13. What is the derivation of much formal play?
14. Describe the child-rearing patterns of the Rajputs of North Delhi.
15. Compare and contrast the biological theories of play set forth by
    Spencer, Hall, and Gross, and the shortcomings of each position.
16. Describe Freud's theory of psychosexual development.
17. What evidence supports Freud's belief that some people fixate at the
    oral or anal stages of development?
18. Describe Freud's theory of the Oedipal and Electra situations, and
    the means by which children resolve them.
19. What is the process of repression and how does it operate during the
    latent period of development?
20. What evidence supports Freud's theory of libidinal energy?
21. Describe the child-rearing practices of the Tairans of Okinawa.
22. Specify the limitations of Freud's and Piaget's theories of child
    development.
23. Discuss the purpose of play as summarized by McConnell.
24. Define the following terms: assimilation, accommodation, ontogeny
    recapitulates phylogeny, sensory-motor period, pre-operational
    stage, stage of concrete operations, stage of formal operations,
    play, social play, formal play, creative play, free play, psycho-
    sexual development, libido, oral stage, anal stage, phallic stage,
    Oedipal situation, Electra situation, repression, latent period,
    genital stage, libidinal energy, fixated.

ACTION PROJECT 22

Testing Thinking Development

According to Piaget, the pre-operational stage exists between the
ages of about 2 to 6. During this stage the child lacks the ability to
understand that changes in the shape or position of an object do not
change its volume or size. The child's mind cannot yet grasp conservation concepts.

It can be great fun giving some of Piaget's tests to pre-school
children. For the conservation of volume test fill two tall, thin
glasses so they both have equal amounts of water. Ask the child: "Do
the glasses contain the same amount of water?" After the child says
"Yes," pour the water from one glass into a larger but shorter glass.
Then repeat the question.

To test conservation of length, place two pencils (or sticks) of
equal length side by side. Ask: "Are the pencils the same length?"
After the child says "Yes," move one pencil closer and one pencil far-
ther back on the table. Repeat the question.

To test conservation of mass, obtain some clay or children's play
dough and form two balls of equal size. Ask: "Is one bigger than the

other?" After the child says "No," flatten one ball and repeat the question.

To test conservation of quantity, arrange two sets of five pennies in lines of equal length. Ask: "Does each line have the same number of pennies?" After the child says "Yes," move the pennies in one line closer together and lengthen the other line. Then repeat the question.

OUTSIDE READING

Bennett, Harold. No More Public School (New York: Random House, Inc., 1972).

Fraiberg, Selma. The Magic Years (New York: Charles Scribner's Sons, 1959).

Montessori, Maria. The Secret of Childhood (New York: Ballantine Books, 1971).

Neil, A.S. Summerhill (New York: Hart Publishing Company, 1966).

Chapter 23

PREDICTING EXAM QUESTIONS

1. According to Freud, what is the purpose of catharsis?

2. How do Freud and Jung view the operation of the unconscious?

3. Name and briefly describe Erik Eriksen's eight stages of psycho-social development.

4. Describe Carl Roger's view of the fully adjusted person.

5. How does Maslow's view of human development differ from traditional psychoanalytic views?

YOUR QUESTIONS

6.

7.

8.

9.

10.

YOUR SUMMARY

TESTING THE TEST

1. T F Personality is the characteristic way in which a person thinks and behaves as he or she adjusts to his or her environment.
2. T F Catharsis is a technique to relieve psychological pain by encouraging people to forget unpleasant experiences.
3. T F Freud divided the psyche into two systems, the conscious and the unconscious.
4. T F During the Oedipal or Electral crisis the child becomes emotionally attached to the parent of the opposite sex.
5. T F Defense mechanisms help the Ego handle demands placed on it by the Id and Superego.
6. T F Identification is the defense mechanism through which the Oedipal and Electral crises are resolved.
7. T F Jung agreed with Freud's notion that the human being's chief task in life is to bring his or her infantile, sexual instincts under control.
8. T F The two major Jungian archtypes are the persona and anima.
9. T F According to Adler, humans have an innate drive for self-realization, for completion, and perfection which is the driving force of life itself.
10. T F B.F. Skinner believes that behavior is, above all else, lawful.

PROVOCATIVE QUESTIONS AND ISSUES

1. If defense mechanisms are used by the Ego to fend off assaults, then should a person try to avoid or stop using defense mechanisms? Does a person with good mental health use defense mechanisms, or not?
2. As a result of your thinking and reading about personality, what are your ideas of a healthy personality?

CHAPTER OBJECTIVES

1. Characterize the job of the personality theorist.
2. What is the purpose of catharsis?
3. According to Freud, what is the pleasure principle and the purpose of the primary process?
4. Describe Freud's reality principle and the purpose of the secondary process of the mind.
5. Give an example of the function of the preconscious.
6. Identify the relationship between the Id and the Libido.
7. How do the following defense mechanisms operate and what characteristics do they have in common: repression, fixation, regression, identification, reaction formation, projection, sublimation, displacement?
8. What function does Freud attribute to the Ego?

9. Compare and contrast the differing views of Freud and Jung regarding the operation of the unconscious.
10. How are the collective and personal unconscious thought to operate?
11. Why did Jung view the Ego as the most important archtype?
12. Describe the function of the persona and anima.
13. What is Jung's theory of polarities?
14. Describe the philosophical differences of Adler and Freud.
15. Describe Eriksen's psychosocial theory of development and indicate the function of each of the eight stages.
16. What is the humanistic philosophy of self-actualization?
17. How does Rogers view the maturation process in humans?
18. What is Rogers' view of the fully-adjusted person?
19. How does Maslow's view of man's development differ from traditional views?
20. Name the two basic needs hypothesized by Maslow.
21. Describe Skinner's philosophy regarding the lawfulness of behavior.
22. Define the following terms: catharsis, pleasure principle, primary process, personality theory, conscious, pre-conscious, unconscious, secondary process, reality principle, Id, Ego, Superego, Libido, defense mechanisms, regression, identification, reaction formation, projection, displacement, sublimation, personal unconscious, collective unconscious, archtypes, persona, animal, introversion, extroversion, creative self, inferiority complex, compensation, psycho-social theory of development, phenomenal field, basic needs, meta-needs.

ACTION PROJECT 23A

Self-actualization

Maslow's observations and descriptions of self-actualized people helped lead to the development of humanistic psychology. This branch of psychology focuses on the processes involved when a person strives to reach full potential. A useful step to take in an effort to develop yourself is to observe and talk with self-developed people.

Arrange to interview three or four people who enjoy being who and what they are, people who are "doing their things" and don't worry much about what people might think of them. According to Maslow some of the characteristics you are likely to find in such persons are:

Perceives reality more accurately than others; can tolerate ambiguity and uncertainty.
Is self-confident; accepts others for what they are.
Is problem-oriented rather than self-centered.
Is spontaneous in thought and action.
Has a need for privacy and can take a detached view of the world.
Is independent, but doesn't challenge convention.
Has a fresh, deep appreciation for people, not a stereotyped view.
Has had a mystic or spiritual experience of deep personal significance.
Has a strong social interest and identifies with mankind.
Has close emotional relationships with a few people
Respects all people in a democratic way.
Distinguishes means from ends and usually enjoys the means.

Sense of humor is philosophical rather than hostile.
Is creative.
Is adapted to the culture but cannot be made to conform.

During your interviews you may find it useful to ask the people to discuss ways in which they are like this list and ways they differ. After you have completed your interviews it can be useful to get together with other students who have done the project and discuss what you learned.

ACTION PROJECT 23B

A Test of Maturity

A mature person should be able to re-examine an old belief when facts supporting a different view are presented to him or her.
Show the statement and picture below to a number of people. How do they handle this idea? Do they miss the point? Do they laugh? Get angry?
In the space beneath the picture keep a record of the various responses you get.
When you are finished, talk over your findings with some friends. Try to see what the responses to this test indicate about a person's personality.

Since white is a mixture of all colors and black is the absence of all colors, the whiter a person's skin is, the more colored he is.

"WHAT IS IT LIKE TO BE COLORED?"

OUTSIDE READING

Freud, Sigmund. A General Introduction to Psychoanalysis (New York: Doubleday & Company, Inc., 1953; originally published in 1920).

Jourard, Sidney M. Personal Adjustment (New York: The Macmillan Company, 1963).

Salter, Andrew. The Case Against Psychoanalysis (New York: Citadel, 1963).

Chapter 24

PREDICTING EXAM QUESTIONS

1. What are the basic differences between the theories of Kretschmer and Sheldon?

2. What is the fallacy in assuming that IQ scores should fit a bell-shaped curve?

3. How are test reliability and validity determined?

4. Why is it difficult to design a reliable or valid IQ test?

5. How may IQ tests present biased data and discriminate against various individuals or groups?

YOUR QUESTIONS

6.

7.

8.

9.

10.

YOUR SUMMARY

TESTING THE TEST

1. T F According to Galen, your biochemistry determines your personality type.
2. T F Kretschmer insists that people do not have to be a pure body type and in many cases are mixtures.
3. T F Binet and Simon devised the first intelligence test in an attempt to identify retarded children in need of special attention.
4. T F Most intelligence tests are based on the assumption that scores should be normally distributed.
5. T F A reliable test is one that measures what it says it measures and measures little or nothing else.
6. T F Your IQ score reflects intellectual capacity, past experience, and your present motivational state.
7. T F Most IQ tests now in use were devised by people who defined intelligence as traits necessary to succeed in all social levels of society.
8. T F Life itself is the best IQ test we presently have available.
9. T F According to McClelland, IQ tests do not measure traits that deal with success in the non-academic world.
10. T F The Rorschach tends to be a highly reliable test.

PROVOCATIVE QUESTIONS AND ISSUES

1. When one of the authors of this manual was working as a psychologist for a juvenile court in a large city the following incident took place: The mother of a teenage girl came to court and signed a petition requesting that her daughter be declared a juvenile delinquent and sent to the state industrial school for delinquents. The mother claimed that the girl consistently refused to obey her, even when threatened with the possibility of being sent to the state school.

   When the case worker investigated he learned that the mother had been told some years previously--when the girl was in grade school--that the girl had an IQ of 140, and that the mother could expect some outstanding accomplishments from her "genius" daughter. The mother later moved to a district which had the best high school in the city. In spite of constant urging and supervision by the mother, however, the girl was only achieving a "B" average in high school. The mother forced the girl to study in the evenings and on weekends, but the girl could do no better than a "B" average in this school where the average IQ of the students was reported to be 124. The mother finally became so enraged at her "genius" daughter refusing to perform at superior levels that she turned to the juvenile authorities to institute "proper" punishment.

   The case worker located the teacher who had told the mother about the 140 IQ in order to determine the facts. It turned out that the teacher had given a typing proficiency test to her class and that this girl had done extremely well. She had obtained a score equal to that of the average 14-year-old even though she was only 10. The teacher, knowing that an IQ is calculated with the formula $MA/CA \times 100$, told the mother at the next Parent-

Teachers meeting that if the girl's other potentials matched her typing potential her IQ must be at least 140, and that the girl could be a genius.

Meanwhile the girl had been given a standard IQ test in the psychological clinic and was found to have a Wechsler Full Scale IQ of 108. The eventual conclusion was that rather than performing below capacity, this girl was earning grades above her capacity in school because of her many hours of hard work and effort.

In view of this case history what is your opinion of the wisdom of school authorities or teachers telling parents or students about IQ scores?

CHAPTER OBJECTIVES

1. How may psychological traits be analyzed in measurable terms?
2. How valid was Galen's humor theory?
3. How useful is Kretschmer's morphological theory?
4. How useful is Sheldon's theory of body types?
5. Identify the basic differences between the theories of Kretschmer and Sheldon.
6. How did Binet and Simon devise their first intelligence test?
7. How were Binet and Simon influenced by Darwin?
8. What was the rationale behind the normal distribution or bell-shaped curve theory?
9. What is the fallacy in assuming that IQ's should fit into a bell-shaped curve?
10. How are test reliability and validity determined?
11. Why is it difficult to design reliable or valid IQ tests?
12. Give several examples of how culture effects intelligence.
13. How does Ertl measure intelligence neurologically?
14. Why is life survival the best measure of intelligence?
15. Describe McClelland's analysis as to why unreliable and invalid IQ tests are still used in schools.
16. What evidence supports Allport's Theory of Traits?
17. Describe Allport's Theory of Values.
18. List the differences between cardinal, central, and secondary traits.
19. How does one administer the word association test and what is its function?
20. Describe the design and function of the Thematic Apperception Test.
21. Describe the function of the Rorschach test, and its reliability and validity as a projective measure.
22. How was the Minnesota Multiphasic Personality Inventory designed, and how reliable and valid is it as a projective measure?
23. List the strengths and weaknesses of the personality scales as tools for psychological help.
24. Identify the ethical considerations one must take into account when using personality inventories and intelligence tests.
25. How may IQ tests present biased data and discriminate against various individuals or groups?
26. Define the following terms: psychological traits, Galen's humor theory, humor, phlegmatic, choleric, sanguine, melancholic, Kretschmer's morphological theory, morphology, pyknic, asthetic, athletic, mesomorphs, ectomorphs, normal distribution, bell-shaped curve, test reliability, operant tests, respondent tests,

Allport's theory of values, Allport's theory of traits, individual traits, common traits, cardinal traits, central traits, secondary traits, objective tests, subjective tests, word association tests, Rorschach, Minnesota Multiphasic Personality Inventory.

ACTION PROJECT 24

An IQ Test

IQ tests were originally developed to help identify which students would benefit the most from advanced schooling. In recent times, however, questions have been raised about whether or not IQ tests are fair.

To help show you what an IQ test is like we have obtained permission from the New English Library, Ltd., to reproduce "Verbal Test A" from the book, How Intelligent Are You? by Victor Serebriakoff, former general secretary of Mensa International. This test is provided for educational purposes only. The norms for scoring are not based on careful statistical analysis and no claims are made as to reliability or validity.

There are 50 items in the test and you have exactly 30 minutes to complete it. The answers and scoring norms are on pages 146-147.

VERBAL TEST A*

Analogies I

There are four terms in analogies. The first is related to the second in the same way that the third is related to the fourth. Complete each analogy by underlining two words from the four in brackets.
Example: high is to low as (sky, earth, tree, plant).
VA 1. sitter is to chair as (cup, saucer, plate, leg).
VA 2. needle is to thread as (cotton, sew, leader, follower).
VA 3. better is to worse as (rejoice, choice, bad, mourn).
VA 4. floor is to support as (window, glass, view, brick).
VA 5. veil is to curtain as (eyes, see, window, hear).

Similarities

Underline the two words in each line with the most similar meanings.
Example: mat, lino, floor, rug.
VA 6. divulge, divert, reveal, revert.
VA 7. blessing, bless, benism, blessed.
VA 8. intelligence, speediness, currents, tidings.
VA 9. tale, novel, volume, story.
VA 10. incarcerate, punish, cane, chastise.

Comprehension

Read this incomplete passage. The spaces in the passage are to be filled by words from the list beneath. In each space write the letter of the word which would most suitably fill the space. No word should be used more than once and some are not needed at all.

---

* © 1968 Victor Serebriakoff. Reprinted with permission.

VA 11 to 20. A successful author is (....) in danger of the (....) of
his fame whether he continues or ceases to (....). The regard of the
(....) is not to be maintained but by tribute, and the (....) of past
service to them will quickly languish (....) some (....) performance
brings back to the rapidly (....) minds of the masses the (....) upon
which the (....) is based.
(A) neither, (B) fame, (C) diminution, (D) public, (E) remembrance,
(F) equally, (G) new, (H) unless, (I) forgetful, (J) unreal, (K) merit,
(L) write.

Odd Out

In each group of words below underline the two words whose meanings
do not belong with the others.
Example: robin, pigeon, spade, fork, eagle.
VA 21. shark, sea lion, cod, whale, plaice.
VA 22. baize, paper, felt, cloth, tinfoil.
VA 23. sword, arrow, dagger, dart, club.
VA 24. microscope, telephone, microphone, telescope, telegraph.
VA 25. stench, fear, sound, warmth, love.

Links

Write in the brackets one word which means the same in one sense as
the word on the left and in another sense the same as the word on the
right.   il
Example: price-list (B**L) beak.
VA 26. dash (D**T) missile.
VA 27. mould (F**M) class.
VA 28. squash (P***S) crowd.
VA 29. thin (F**E) good.
VA 30. ignite (F**E) shoot.

Opposites

In each line below underline the two words that are most nearly
opposite in meaning.
Example: heavy, large, light.
VA 31. insult, deny, denigrate, firm, affirm.
VA 32. missed, veil, confuse, secret, expose.
VA 33. frank, overt, plain, simple secretive.
VA 34. aggravate, please, enjoy, improve, like.
VA 35. antedate, primitive, primordial, primate, ultimate.

Mid-terms

In each line, three terms on the right should correspond with three
terms on the left. Insert the missing mid-term on the right.

Example: first (second) third:: one (T-wo-) three.
VA 36. past (Present) future:: was (I----) will be.
VA 37. complete (Incomplete) blank:: always (S----) never.
VA 38. glut (Scarcity) famine:: many (F----) none.
VA 39. rushing (Passing) enduring:: evanescent (T----T) eternal.
VA 40. nascent (Mature) senile:: green (R----) decayed.

Opposite or Similar

In each line below underline two words which mean most nearly Either the opposite Or the same as each other.

Examples: (a) mat, lino, rug, (b) hate, affection, love.

VA 41. rapport, mercurial, happy, rapacious, phlegmatic.

VA 42. object, deter, demur, defer, oblate.

VA 43. tenacious, resolve, irresolute, solution, tenacity.

VA 44. real, renal, literally, similarly, veritably.

VA 45. topography, menhir, prime, plateau, cleft

Analogies II

Complete each analogy by writing one word in the brackets ending with the letters printed.

Example: high is to low as sky is to (----TH). [ear above TH]

VA 46. proud is to humble as generous is to (----H).

VA 47. brave is to fearless as daring is to (----ID).

VA 48. lend is to borrow as harmony is to (----D).

VA 49. rare is to common as remote is to (----NT).

VA 50. skull is to brain as shell is to (----K).

Answers to Verbal Test A

VA 1. cup, saucer. VA 2. leader, follower (in the operation of sewing, the thread follows the needle). VA 3. rejoice, mourn (opposites). VA 4. window, view (a floor provides support and a window provides a view). VA 5. eyes, window (veils cover eye as curtains cover windows). VA 6. divulge, reveal. VA 7. blessing, benism. VA 8. intelligence, tidings ('intelligence' in the sense of 'news'). VA 9. tale, story. VA 10. punish, chastise. VA 11. F (equally). VA 12. C (diminution). VA 13. L (write). VA 14. D (public). VA 15. E (remembrance). VA 16. H (unless). VA 17. G (new). VA 18. I (forgetful). VA 19. K (merit). VA 20. B (fame). VA 21. sea lion, whale (both mammals, the others are fish). VA 22. cloth and tinfoil (the others are made of compressed fibres). VA 23. arrow, dart (the others are used in the hand). VA 24. telephone, telegraph (the others increase the object). VA 25. love, fear (the others are detected by the senses). VA 26. dart. VA 27. form. VA 28. press. VA 29. fine. VA 30. fire. VA 31. deny, affirm. VA 32. veil, expose. VA 33. frank, secretive. VA 34. aggravate, improve. VA 35. primordial, ultimate. VA 36. is. VA 37. sometimes. VA 38. few. VA 39. transient. VA 40. ripe. VA 41. mercurial, phlegmatic (opposites). VA 42. object, demur (synonyms). VA 43. tenacious, irresolute (opposites). VA 44. literally, veritably (synonyms). VA 45. menhir, cleft (synonyms). VA 46. selfish. VA 47. intrepid. VA 48. discord. VA 49. present. VA 50. yolk.

Marks	Quotients
0- 5	85- 95
6-12	96-105
13-18	106-112
19-25	113-118
26-30	119-122
31-35	123-128
36-40	129-131
41-45	132-137
46-49	138-140+

A mark of about 40 on this test might indicate that a person would stand a good chance of obtaining Mensa membership after more thorough testing.

Mensa is an international organization whose sole qualification for membership is that one place at the 98th percentile or higher on a standard IQ test. For information about Mensa and the procedures for taking supervised IQ tests write to American Mensa Selection Agency, P.O. Box 86-S, Brooklyn, New York 11223.

OUTSIDE READING

You can obtain a fascinating and informative view of the tests psychologists use by going to the library reference section and looking through the Mental Measurements Yearbook edited by Boros.
  Whaley, Donald. Psychological Testing and the Philosophy of
    Measurement (Kalamazoo, Mich.: Behaviordelia, Inc., 1972).

Chapter 25

PREDICTING EXAM QUESTIONS

1. How is the average score on an IQ test determined?

2. What are the differences between the mean, median, and mode?

3. According to the psychoanalytic point of view, what are the six main types of neuroses?

4. What is Eysenck's theory on the development of neurotic symptoms?

5. What is the difference between an organic psychosis and a functional psychosis?

YOUR QUESTIONS

6.

7.

8.

9.

10.

YOUR SUMMARY

TESTING THE TEST

1. T F To find the mean of a distribution you add up all the scores
           and divide by the number of people who took the test.
2. T F John Kargas has found a marked decrease in IQ scores as
           people grow older.
3. T F Senile psychosis is often due to hardening of the arteries.
4. T F A neurosis is a more severe intrapsychic abnormality than a
           psychosis.
5. T F Eysenck states that there are two basic personality dimen-
           sions, introversion-extroversion and abnormal-neurotic.
6. T F Eysenck believes that all neurotic symptoms are learned.
7. T F The least common of the functional psychoses is schizophrenia.
8. T F People suffering from affective psychoses appear to be stuck
           at one end of the emotionality scale or the other.
9. T F Social disorders are more likely to cause problems to others
           than to the person who shows the deviant behavior.
10. T F Kinsey's data suggest that few adults engage in occasional
           homosexual behavior.

PROVOCATIVE QUESTIONS AND ISSUES

1. If you had your choice, would you be most pleased to hear that you
     had obtained an IQ score of 130 on the Wechsler Adult Intelligence
     Scale or an IQ of 135 on the Cattell Intelligence Test? Would
     your choice be influenced by the fact that the standard deviation
     for WAIS scores is 15 and the standard deviation for Cattell
     scores is 23?
         When the standard deviations are taken into account it means
     that a WAIS score of 130 is about 2 standard deviations above the
     mean and that this is a much better score than a Cattell score of

135, which is only about 1½ standard deviations above the mean. What do you think psychologists should do about a situation where different IQ tests have different standard deviations? Does this information help explain why Mensa bases its membership scores on percentile placement rather than on IQ score?

CHAPTER OBJECTIVES

1. How would a mental patient differ from the average citizen?
2. What is the significance of Kinsey's data on the sexual activity of males?
3. How is the average score on an IQ test determined?
4. Describe the difference between the mean, median, and mode.
5. Why does the mean often present a distorted picture?
6. How is the standard deviation determined?
7. What is the significance of Kangas's research into the sexual performance of elderly Americans?
8. What are the symptoms of senile psychosis, and what methods are used to prevent or treat it?
9. List the factors which cause general paresis.
10. What is the relationship between psychoses and neurosis?
11. Identify the five stages in the development of a neurosis.
12. Describe the six types of neurosis from the psychoanalytic point of view.
13. Why does Eysenck view neuroses as learned phenomena?
14. Describe Eysenck's introversion-extroversion dimension.
15. List the main types of schizophrenia and their basic behavioral characteristics.
16. What are the behavioral characteristics of the manic and depressive psychotic?
17. Describe the difference between people who have neuroses, psychoses, and social disorders.
18. How are transvestism and homosexual behavior encouraged by parents?
19. Why do people undertake the following deviate sexual behaviors: pedophilia, voyeurism, exhibitionism, bestiality, fetishism, satyrism, and nymphomania?
20. What is the significance of Kinsey's analysis regarding the frequency of deviant sexual behavior among American males?
21. Give several examples of anti-social and deviant behavior that are multi-determined.
22. Define the following terms: satyr, mode, median, mean, norm, standard deviation, prostate, stroke, senile psychosis, general paresis, alcohol psychosis, drug-induced psychosis, intra-psychic, neurosis, psycho-neurosis, psychoses, conversion reaction, depressive reaction, obsessive-compulsive reaction, phobic reaction, anxiety reaction, dissociative reaction, introversion-extroversion, functional psychosis, schizophrenia, dementia praecox, simple schizophrenia, hebephrenic schizophrenia, catatonic schizophrenia, paranoid schizophrenia, affective psychoses, affective reactions, manic psychosis, depressive psychosis, transvestism, homosexual, lesbian, pedophilia, voyeur, exhibitionist, bestiality, fetishism, satyrism, nymphomania, perverse.

ACTION PROJECT 25

Introversion-extroversion Test

One of the personality dimensions frequently examined is that of
introversion-extroversion. Numerous studies have shown that this is not
a simple dimension to evaluate, however, because a person can be intro-
verted in some ways and extroverted in others. To give you a rough idea
of what tendencies are assessed in introversion-extroversion measures,
we have made up this test for you to take. Scoring instructions and some
norms are on the next page. Keep in mind that this test is for instruc-
tional purposes only and should not be viewed as a valid measure of your
personality.

Instructions

Look at each pair of statements below and mark the one statement
which applies to you more than the other.

1. a. _____ do not belong to many clubs or groups.
   b. _____ enjoy being in clubs and groups.
2. a. _____ outgoing, sociable.
   b. _____ shy, modest.
3. a. _____ would like a public-relations job.
   b. _____ would rather be a computer operator.
4. a. _____ dislike being teased.
   b. _____ being teased is part of the fun of being with others.
5. a. _____ enjoy a good argument at times.
   b. _____ hate to get into any kind of argument.
6. a. _____ plan ahead for most social activities.
   b. _____ seldom plan ahead; do most things on the spur of the moment.
7. a. _____ enjoy a big, noisy party.
   b. _____ prefer a quiet time with a good friend.
8. a. _____ self-conscious, embarrass easily.
   b. _____ rarely get embarrassed; don't think about self much.
9. a. _____ at parties sit by self or wander around watching and
           listening.
   b. _____ mix well at parties; tend to be in the center of the action.
10. a. _____ talking with strangers an effort; have trouble making
            conversation.
    b. _____ don't think of people as strangers; talk easily to most
            people.
11. a. _____ shrug off criticism easily; forget it happened.
    b. _____ tend to brood over criticism; mind dwells on ways to answer
            back.
12. a. _____ rarely initiate activities with others.
    b. _____ often organize friends to do things.
13. a. _____ need to spend time away from others thinking and daydreaming.
    b. _____ too active doing things to have time for daydreaming.
14. a. _____ persistent; good at jobs requiring a lot of detail work.
    b. _____ dislike wasting time on small details; prefer leaving that
            to others.
15. a. _____ seldom irritated by other people; quickly show feelings when
            angered.
    b. _____ often irritated by others, but hide reactions.

16. a. _____ moral standards are higher than those of the average person; this is an important concern.

    b. _____ moral standards about the same as everyone else's; not a concern of great importance.

17. a. _____ sometimes enjoy dressing in ways that will cause some heads to turn.

    b. _____ dress to look nice, but dislike being stared at.

18. a. _____ believe that success in a career will come mainly from educational accomplishments.

    b. _____ believe that success in a career will depend mainly on ability to get along with people.

19. a. _____ would rather present ideas to a group using a printed handout.

    b. _____ would rather present ideas to a group in the form of a talk.

20. a. _____ rarely spend time thinking about how to talk to someone.

    b. _____ often mentally rehearse what will be said to someone.

21. a. _____ will be reluctant to let others see the score obtained on this test.

    b. _____ want to compare score on this test with friends' scores.

Scoring Key for Introversion-Extroversion Test

Calculate your <u>introversion</u> score by counting how many of the following you chose:

1. a	8. a	15. b	Extroversion = 21 minus
2. b	9. a	16. a	Introversion
3. b	10. a	17. b	
4. a	11. b	18. a	
5. b	12. a	19. a	
6. a	13. a	20. b	
7. b	14. a	21. a	

Total: _____

During the pre-test 142 students obtained a Mean Introversion score of 9.5 with a standard deviation of 3.4. The range was from a low of 3 to a high of 18.

OUTSIDE READINGS

Fromm, Erich. <u>The Sane Society</u> (New York: Holt, Rinehart and Winston, Inc., 1955).

Ullmann, Leonard P., and Leonard Krasner. <u>A Psychological Approach to Abnormal Behavior</u> (Englewood Cliffs, N.J.: Prentice-Hall, Inc., 1969).

Chapter 26

PREDICTING EXAM QUESTIONS

1. What is the "devil theory" of mental illness? Give several examples.

2. Describe the positive and negative effects of psycho-surgery.

3. What conclusions did Werner Mendel reach regarding the effectiveness
   of psychotherapy?

4. What are the six main advantages in using group psychotherapy?

5. Describe the theoretical basis of token economies and the reasons
   for their relative successes.

YOUR QUESTIONS

6.

7.

8.

9.

10.

YOUR SUMMARY

TESTING THE TEST

1. T F During electro-shock therapy the patient goes into convulsions
         similar to those of an epileptic.
2. T F Werner Mendel found that reserpine had a dramatic effect on
         the behavior of psychotic patients.
3. T F Most personality theorists believe that abnormal thoughts are
         mere symptoms of underlying personality dysfunction.
4. T F Transference is the method by which analysts prevent strong
         emotional dependency between themselves and their patients.
5. T F Free association is the basic game plan of most forms of
         psychoanalysis.

6. T F According to Maslow and Rogers, therapy should consist primarily of making the individual aware of his present state of functioning.

7. T F Eysenck reported that the improvement rate of patients given no form of therapy was better than those given psychotherapy.

8. T F Greenspoon's research demonstrated that therapists seldom reward patients for "sick talk."

9. T F Recent studies of group therapy indicate that there is much scientific evidence that group therapy is of considerable value.

10. T F Socio-behavioral therapists tend to see mental illness as being caused by unhealthy living conditions.

PROVOCATIVE QUESTIONS AND ISSUES

1. Can you imagine a situation in which it might seem reasonable for a doctor to recommend suicide to someone who has a "psychiatric" problem? Read the following story, show it to several friends, and then try to form an opinion about how justified the doctor was.

THE RAPIST WHO TOOK MY ADVICE

Charles F. Mourland, M.D.*

Technically, I guess, I could be considered an accessory to murder. After more than 20 years, I still wonder whether I should have done something different. What would you have done? Anyway, this was the problem, and I'll let you decide for yourself:

World War II was drawing to a close, and I was finishing my internship at a large general hospital. Gas rationing and a manpower shortage were wartime facts. The first was unpleasant, but the girls made the manpower shortage delightful, if you happened to be young, single, draft-deferred, and a newly graduated M.D. From my job as intern on the psycho ward, I went to the beach on all free afternoons, having a few more gas ration coupons than the average collegian. During my sojourns at the beach, I got to know all the other regulars--most of them either college girls or male graduate students, deferred like me.

The foremost exception to this collegiate conglomerate was a character nicknamed "Snake" because of his peculiar, unblinking reptilian stare. Going from my locked-ward work with psychotics directly to play, I couldn't help but observe him with great professional interest because he was different. Snake was a product of a fine, old-rich family from one of the nearby conservative old residential towns. For generations, his family had had both money and social position. His father was a high-ranking Army officer.

Snake himself had been the promising scion of this upper-class family until about the age of 16. Handsome and bright, he'd always done well in school. He had all the polish that inherited wealth could give him. He'd been a fine all-around athlete and a particularly skillful amateur boxer. I learned later that at age 16, seven years before I met him, he suddenly changed. Instead of leading his class, he repeatedly flunked. He was later kicked out of several colleges for various kinds of trouble. When he finally got medical rather than disciplinary treatment, he was diagnosed as having some strange variety of schizophrenia. By this time, his father was away at war, and his doting mother couldn't or wouldn't accept such a diagnosis. After all, Snake was her baby boy; nothing really serious could be wrong with him!

Despite his mental condition, Snake was eventually drafted into the service. But his career was abruptly terminated after about a year, when he was court-martialed for rape--three different counts, three different girls. His guilt was accepted without question, and he was discharged from the service for civilian treatment. He wasn't punished because the court-martial board felt that he was obviously psychotic. After his discharge, he would hitchhike or drive his convertible (when he could get enough gas coupons) to the beach every day, in uniform.

At the beach, I was fascinated by Snake's effect on the girls from two of our enlightened colleges. These girls were against all Establishment things and just as rebellious as college youngsters are now. But when Snake walked among them, their sophisticated poses broke up into absolute panic. They weren't just a little cool--they were terrified, as frightened of him as they would have been if a cobra had wandered into their midst. The reason for their fear was widely known. Snake, I discovered, was in the habit of picking up girls, very easy for anyone in uniform during World War II. But he didn't merely pick them up for companionship. He'd then beat them and rape them. In fact, he raped a couple of girls every week.

Though I've known many psychotics since then and criminals--not to mention actors--I've never seen anyone who projected the aura of menace that Snake did. Several times, without provocation, I saw him fly into homicidal, literally mouth-foaming rages. He was as frightening to look at as a mad dog. I'd marvel at how much more dangerous Snake was than the people I'd just left in locked wards, and usually in restraints, at the hospital.

Shortly before I'd met him, Snake had been in jail for five weeks. Nancy, the girl whose complaint had put him there, later told me about it. In spite of all the jokes about how a girl can't be raped, Nancy had been. She'd known Snake from the days when they were school kids together, before he'd changed. She wasn't afraid of him. One afternoon, after years of not seeing him, she met him at the swimming pool of a big hotel. He asked her for a date for that night, and she gladly accepted. During dinner, he was his normal charming self, just as he'd been years before when she'd been out with him. After dinner they drove away. He parked his convertible and immediately started to take off her pants. She demurred. So he blackened her eyes, loosened her teeth, strangled her into insensibility, ripped off her clothes, and raped her. Dazed and hysterical, she walked five miles to her home.

The next morning, her brother looked into her bedroom to see why she hadn't come down for breakfast. He noticed her bruised face, and she told him what had happened. He roused their parents and said he was going to kill Snake, but they talked him out of it and notified the district attorney instead. The D.A. acted on Nancy's complaint of assault and battery. (Unmarried girls, I'm told, will almost never sign a complaint of rape.) Snake was arrested and jailed. Snake's mother then called Nancy and told her that Snake had been diagnosed as a schizo-phrenic. Mother said that if Nancy would withdraw her complaint, Mother would see to it that Snake received treatment. Nancy agreed.

So Nancy called the district attorney and asked to withdraw her complaint. But he refused to let her do so, saying that she was the third girl in that town to file a similar complaint against Snake. At his trial, photographs taken of Nancy after her beating were shown, and Snake got a maximum term of six months for assault and battery. In about five weeks, though, thanks to Mother and her good lawyers, he was out again and back at the beach every day.

Obviously, Snake wasn't sane during critical times. Much of the time, however, he was rational, intelligent, charming, and really quite a nice fellow. He'd often talk to me, and I learned that his one great pride was his family--their name and reputation. Because of that and the fact that he didn't want to hurt them any more, he sought my help as a physician. "I know there's something the matter with me," he'd say. "Something comes over me. I believe I'm really insane. What do you think I ought to do?"

My initial advice to him was that he seek treatment for schizophrenia. Treatment at that time consisted almost solely of shock therapy. But Snake said that he'd already had that--16 or 24 or 32 jolts in the service and since--and it had done nothing for him. I next suggested that he commit himself voluntarily to a mental institution, permanently. He agreed that sooner or later he was going to do something too bad for Mother's money and influence to hush up--such as killing one of those girls that he beat up so badly. He refused to commit himself because he liked to go to the beach, he said. He didn't want to be in prison, even though prison was called an asylum.

In desperation, I blurted out my third suggestion to Snake. To spare his family further disgrace, I urged him to commit suicide. This time he had no comment. A few days later, Snake drove his beautiful convertible off a cliff and killed himself.

Several questions raised by Snake's suicide and my part in it still plague me. Had my advice been medically and ethically immoral? Or was Snake so far gone that the end justified the means? How many rights have other members of society? How much psychological and physical damage did the many others whom he'd beaten and raped suffer? Where did their rights begin, and his end? When I recall the wild sobbing and the hys-terical abreaction that Nancy had had when she told me how Snake had beaten her, I can't help but believe that her <u>rights</u> had been violated.

If you believe that I did give the wrong advice when I was asked for it, what should I have done differently? How can society best defend itself against such pitiful but dangerously sick persons? Was there a better answer then? Is there a better answer now? What advice would <u>you</u> have given in the same circumstances?

CHAPTER OBJECTIVES

1. What is the basis for the "devil theory" of mental illness?
2. Describe the psychosis known as witigo and the treatment thought to be its cure.
3. List the behavioral characteristics of running amok.
4. What is the Chinese phobia called koro and the treatment prescribed as its cure?

5. Identify the pertinent issues which must be raised in evaluating forms of therapy.
6. How is electro-shock therapy administered, and what is its cure rate?
7. Discuss the theory behind sleep therapy.
8. Describe the various forms of psycho-surgery and their positive and negative effects.
9. What is the basis for the use of tranquilizers as a means of treatment and how effective are they for curing psychological problems?
10. Describe the use of sugar pills in Mendel's experimentation with mental patients, and the factors which facilitated their curative powers.
11. Why do psychotherapists believe that curing the patient's symptoms is insufficient?
12. Compare and contrast the two major forms of intra-psychic therapy—psychoanalytic and humanistic—and cite the major differences between them.
13. List the basic goals of psychoanalytic therapy.
14. What is the purpose of transference and free association?
15. Describe the philosophy upon which Roger's client-centered therapy is based.
16. How do psychoanalytic and humanistic psychologists evaluate their therapy? Cite the relative effectiveness of each.
17. Summarize the data presented by Eysenck in 1952 regarding the effectiveness of psychotherapy.
18. List the conclusions of the American Psychoanalytic Association's research regarding the effectiveness of psychotherapy.
19. Summarize Mendel's study on the effectiveness of psychotherapy.
20. Why could an untrained psychiatric aide be more effective as a therapist than a psychiatrist?
21. What is the significance of Greenspoon's studies on the effect of therapist attitudes on patient behavior change?
22. List the advantages of using group psychotherapy versus other forms of psychotherapy.
23. What are the basic goals of non-directive group psychotherapy?
24. How is psychodrama designed to help patients?
25. Describe the philosophy behind transactional analysis.
26. List some of the objectives of Gestalt therapy.
27. Describe the objectives of sensitivity training.
28. Summarize the basic goals of encounter groups.
29. What is the significance of Lieberman's, Miles', and Yalom's work on the effectiveness of different types of group therapy?
30. Describe the theoretical basis of environmental therapy.
31. Why have token economies been relatively successful?
32. Why must we analyze all points of view when attempting to determine the form of treatment which is best for the patient?
33. Describe Meyer's holistic approach to analyzing patient problems and treatment needs.
34. Define the following terms: "devil theory" of mental illness, witigo, running amok, koro, shook yong, electro-shock therapy, retrograde amnesia, sleep therapy, psycho-surgery, reserpine, chlorpromazine, serotonin, double-blind, psychoanalytic therapy, transference, free association, humanistic therapy, client-centered therapy, ecletic, group therapy, milieu therapy, psychodrama, transactional analysis, Gestalt therapy, encounter groups, environmental therapy, token economies, holistic.

ACTION PROJECT 26

The Therapy of Friendship

There are times when just talking troubles over with a friend can make you feel good. If one of your friends needs to talk to you about something bothering him or her and you want to be as helpful as possible here are a few useful guidelines. Concentrate on these suggestions, but remember that you are not a professional therapist.

Be a good listener. Listen with your eyes, your mind, and your feelings. Ask for clarification if there's something you don't understand. This will help you and your friend put together an accurate picture and will probably help clarify your friend's thinking.

Show empathy and understanding. Show that you understand the feelings being expressed as well as the words spoken. After all, this is a friend. Comments such as: "That must have made you furious!" or "How did you feel after that?" will keep you in touch with the emotions being expressed.

Summarize and reflect back. By summarizing and saying back to the person what you understand him or her to have been saying, you make certain that you do understand and the friend gains more objectivity.

Let the person talk it through. Just being able to tell someone about what is happening is often enough to help. No suggestions or guidance are called for. If you have a suggestion to make first ask, "May I make a suggestion?" If your friend says no then keep quiet. It is better to err in the direction of saying too little than in saying too much.

Keep the friend feeling responsible. Keep in mind that your friend is responsible for handling this situation and must learn how to deal with such events better in the future. If you take over the problem-solving this will keep your friend weak and tend to encourage dependency on others. Try a line of questioning like this:

"What are you going to do now?
"I don't know."
"What have you tried?"
"I was going to write a letter but gave up on that."
"What else could you do?"

The best solution will be the one that your friend thinks up, not the one that you suggest. After all, your friend must live with the consequences of what he or she does.

Use common sense. Don't try to be a therapist. Be a good, understanding friend and if you sense that the problem is more serious than your friend can handle get the friend to go to a professional for help.

OUTSIDE READING

Ayllon, Teodoro, and Nathan Azrin. The Token Economy: A Motiva-
  tional System for Therapy and Rehabilitation (New York: Appleton-
  Century-Crofts, Inc., 1968).
Balt, John. By Reason of Insanity (New York: New American Library,
  1966).
Green, Hannah. I Never Promised You a Rose Garden (New York: Holt,
  Rinehart and Winston, Inc., 1964).
Stefan, Gregory. In Search of Sanity (New Hyde Park, N.Y.:
  University Books, Inc., 1965).
Szasz, Thomas S. The Myth of Mental Illness (New York: Dell
  Publishing Company, Inc., 1961).
_____ Law, Liberty, and Psychiatry: An Inquiry into the
  Social Uses of Mental Health Practices (New York: The Macmillan
  Company, 1963).

Chapter 27

PREDICTING EXAM QUESTIONS

1. What types of group members received high ratings in Bales' research
    on group problem-solving?

2. How did psychologist Harold Kelly influence his students' attitudes
    toward a class lecturer?

3. What factors influence the size of your personal space?

4. According to Albert Bandura, how may modeling be used as a form of therapy?

5. Describe Byrne's research regarding the major factor attracting one person to another.

YOUR QUESTIONS

6.

7.

8.

9.

10.

TESTING THE TEST

1. T F The role of the task specialist is to praise people for a good performance and smooth over arguments.
2. T F Attitude refers to inconsistent ways of thinking about, feeling toward, or responding to some aspect of your environment.
3. T F Stereotypes are biased attitudes of people toward certain types or groups of people.
4. T F Newcomb's concept of autistic hostility suggests that getting off on the right foot with a new acquaintance isn't really that important.
5. T F An individual's looks and movements typically have a primacy effect in determining initial attitudes toward him or her.
6. T F The most flagrant violation of personal space comes when someone touches us.
7. T F Laing states that schizophrenic patients often increase their rate of eye contact with their peers.
8. T F A social role is a stereotyped set of responses that a person makes to related or similar situations.
9. T F Modeling appears to be the least effective means of behavioral change used by Bandura in curing snake phobia.
10. T F Kelly's studies indicate that opposites do attract but not for long.

PROVOCATIVE QUESTIONS AND ISSUES

1. You know that it is possible to like someone without loving them, but do you believe that it is possible to love someone without liking them? The young man who sent this verse to his girl friend seems to be having this experience:

> There is one feeling beyond
> the deep love I have for you.
> It is my growing awareness that
> I'm beginning to like you too!"

Do you know of any instances where the couple fell in love, but didn't seem to like each other very much? What do you think is the difference between what causes feelings of love and feelings of liking? Can you understand what a woman means when she says that she and her boy friend are "in like"?

CHAPTER OBJECTIVES

1. How could you measure the difference between liking and loving?
2. What is the significance of Bales' research on respect and affection?
3. What are the roles of the task specialist and the social-emotional specialist?
4. How are the various dimensions of attitudes measured?
5. Summarize the research and conclusions of Kelley on the importance of reputations and stereotypes.
6. How are initial impressions often colored by stereotypes?
7. How did Newcomb develop the concept of autistic hostility?
8. Summarize Asch' research and conclusions on the primacy effect.
9. Describe the research and conclusions of Jones on the primacy effect.
10. Give an example of the relationship between non-verbal communication and the primacy effect.
11. How do social expectations of sex, age, and physical characteristics influence the impressions individuals develop of others?
12. What evidence supports the concept of personal space?
13. How does eye contact affect first impressions?
14. What is the significance of the research of Exline on the effects of direct eye contact.
15. Describe the research and conclusions of Jones on the effects of appropriate and inappropriate behaviors on initial impressions.
16. List the characteristics of a social role.
17. Describe the research and conclusions of Backman and Secord on role portrayal, role selection, and fashioning effect.
18. How is transactional analysis used as a form of role-analysis therapy?
19. List the important conclusions of Strickland's research on male and female roles.
20. Give several examples of how people undertake new roles as the situational demands change throughout their lives.
21. Describe Bandura's research and conclusions on learning adaptive roles as a means of therapeutic intervention.
22. Describe the research and conclusions of Byrne on the economics of role-playing.
23. What is the significance of Kelly's research on similarity of marital partners?
24. Define the following terms: social-emotional specialist, task specialist, reputations, attitude, autistic hostility, stereotypes, primacy effect, personal space, social role, role portrayal, role selection, fashioning effect, archtype, transactional analysis, token economy.

ACTION PROJECT 27

How to Influence Attraction and Win Friends

The feelings we have for others are influenced by principles of cause and effect the same as are all human behaviors. Research into feelings of friendship indicates that a main determinant is frequency of contact.

You can check this out for yourself by finding a dormitory where students cannot choose their neighbors, and asking a few of the residents to make up a list of their closest friends. After each list is completed, determine how close each friend's room is to the room of the person who made up the list.

You should find that the people listed as friends are mostly those with whom the person has frequent contact in the dorm. This means that most feelings of friendship are for roommates and people who live close by on the same floor. People whose rooms are near the elevator, stairway, and washroom usually appear on the lists more than people who have rooms at the ends of the hall.

Another way to test the effects of frequency of contact is to pick someone that you don't know well and make an effort to have a number of brief contacts with this person. Don't be overly friendly or attempt to force conversation at first. Just nod, say "hello" and move on. Later, when it seems natural, pause for a moment to ask a question or make a comment, and then leave. If you handle yourself in a controlled, pleasant, and sincere way, you should find feelings of friendship developing between you. With practice you will be able to choose people you want as friends and develop the friendships you want.

OUTSIDE READINGS

Fromm, Erich. The Art of Loving (New York: Harper and Row, 1956; Bantam Books, Inc., 1963, paperback).

Chapter 28

PREDICTING EXAM QUESTIONS

1. How would you determine whether a group existed according to the definition given by McConnell?

2. How would you determine whether a group was homogeneous in their attitudes toward sexual behavior?

3. How is group commitment measured?

4. According to Harold Kelly, how do reference groups influence our
   behavior?

5. According to the Adaptation-level Theory, how is all behavior
   influenced?

YOUR QUESTIONS

6.

7.

8.

9.

10.

TESTING THE TEST

1. T F A group is a collection of two or more people who are psycho-
logically related but are not dependent on one another.
2. T F The major characteristic of any group is the shared acceptance
of an individual's independence by all group members.
3. T F Cohesion is seldom a function of the homogeneity of a group.
4. T F In general, the more you must pay to attain entry into a
group, the greater the rewards will seem to be, and the less
likely it is that you will abandon membership.
5. T F Asch was able to demonstrate that it is extremely difficult
to get people to conform to reference groups.
6. T F According to Adaptation-level Theory, all behavior is influenced by stimulus, background, and personality factors.
7. T F In Milgram's experiments, subjects were more likely to deliver
severe punishment if they couldn't see the consequences of
their actions.
8. T F In general, the vaguer the stimulus, the easier it is to get
the subject to yield in group pressure experiments.
9. T F The more out in the open the subject is forced to be in making
his or her judgments, the less likely it is the subject will
yield to group pressures.
10. T F If a subject is an expert in the task at hand, conformity
pressures are increased in group pressure experiments.

PROVOCATIVE QUESTIONS AND ISSUES

1. If you belong to an organization or group which could be called a
super-organism, does this organism exist for your good or do you
exist for its good? How does a super-organism maintain its
existence?
2. Taking into account the Sherif research into the forces that lead
to inter-group conflict and inter-group cohesion, how would you
explain the dictum that "What this country needs is a good war"
sometimes advocated by political leaders and rulers of nations?

166

CHAPTER OBJECTIVES

1. Identify the characteristics of a group.
2. How would a general systems theorist view a human being?
3. List the function of group rules and their effect on an individual's behavior.
4. Identify the factors which influence the cohesiveness of groups.
5. What is the effect of group commitment on group cohesiveness?
6. How is group commitment measured?
7. Name the important factors affecting group commitment.
8. Describe Aronson's and Mill's research and conclusions on group commitment.
9. What is the significance of Kelley's research on the means by which reference groups influence human behavior?
10. How did Sherif demonstrate the effect of group pressure on visual perception?
11. Describe Asch' research and conclusions on the effect of group pressure on visual perception.
12. How does Helson explain conformity behavior by reference to Adaptation-level Theory?
13. How do the physical properties of a stimulus affect the degree to which a person will yield to group pressures?
14. How do situational variables influence individuals in yielding to group pressures?
15. What effect do personality factors have in influencing individuals to yield to group pressures?
16. Give an example of the phenomenon of negative conformity.
17. Describe Milgram's research and conclusions on conformity.
18. Describe Sherif's research and conclusions on conflict between groups.
19. Define the following terms: social group, social psychology, cohesiveness, commitment, reference groups, Adaptation-level Theory, negative conformity, stimulus variables, situational variables.

ACTION PROJECT 28

Staging with Stooges

This project is the replication of a social psychology experiment. Its purpose is to show you how much a stooge's behavior can influence whether or not people will sign a petition.

For your petition choose a reasonably legitimate topic which people are not likely to have a strong opinion about one way or the other. Pick a topic such as "Petition to have more food vending machines in the school," or "Petition requesting better lighting in school hallways."

When you are ready, take a friend who has volunteered to be a stooge for you and find a place where a few students are likely to walk by. Pick a spot where there is light rather than heavy foot traffic. Have your stooge positioned a distance away from you and then, when a target subject is selected, the stooge is to walk toward you and sign the petition in view of the subject. Practice this several times so that the subject will see you stop the stooge, see the stooge nod "yes" and sign the petition, and then move on before the target subject reaches you.

Then ask the subject to sign the petition.

Do this ten times with the stooge nodding "yes" and signing; ten times with the stooge responding "no" and not signing; and ten times with no stooge present. If you conduct this experiment skillfully, you should obtain evidence which shows why people who circulate petitions sometimes have fake names written into the first few spaces before attempting to get legitimate signatures.

OUTSIDE READING

Frank, Jerome. Sanity and Survival: Psychological Aspects of War and Peace (New York: Random House, Inc., 1967).

Whyte, William, Jr. The Organization Man (New York: Simon and Schuster, Inc., 1956).

Chapter 29

PREDICTING EXAM QUESTIONS

1. In Newcomb's study of college students, what effect did reference groups have on political attitudes?

2. What are the four main factors of persuasive communication?

3. What is the sleeper effect of propaganda communications?

4. What are the main characteristics of effective propaganda?

5. Why did the Cincinnati campaign fail? What could have been done to avoid failure?

6.

7.

8.

9.

10.

YOUR SUMMARY

TESTING THE TEST

1. T F The average American encounters well over 500 ads each day of his life.
2. T F Attitudes often involve bias or pre-judging on our part.
3. T F Newcomb found that the less prestige a woman had among her fellow students, the more likely it was that she was liberal in her views.
4. T F According to Asch, attitude change seldom comes about because of some change in the object of the attitude.
5. T F The audience-communicator feedback loop is perhaps the least studied aspect of the communication process.
6. T F According to the studies of Hovland and Weiss, we tend to move away from the position of someone we mistrust.
7. T F Credibility is crucial in getting information through to the audience.
8. T F Many experiments have shown that high fear propaganda often has the exact long-term effect the communicator hoped for.
9. T F The Star-Hughes study demonstrates that ignorance is the best defense against attitude change.
10. T F Scott found that rewards and punishments had considerable influence on changing attitude.

PROVOCATIVE QUESTIONS AND ISSUES

1. Many advertising people are skilled at influencing the behavior of large numbers of people. What are your thoughts about what right they have to influence people? What right do they have to use their talents to get a politician elected? What are the reasons for and against the use of advertising people by political candidates?

CHAPTER OBJECTIVES

1. What is the relationship between attitudes and memory?
2. Summarize Newcomb's research and conclusions on reference groups and attitude change.
3. Describe Asch's theory regarding the basic ways to induce attitude change.
4. Give examples of the four main factors involved in the communication process.
5. Summarize the research and conclusions of Hovland and Janis on the influence of credibility on attitude change.
6. Give an illustration of the sleeper effect discovered by Hovland and Weiss.
7. Describe the research and conclusions of Heutmann on the value of emotional versus logical appeals.
8. Summarize the research and conclusions of Janis and Fishbach on the effects of fear-arousing communications.
9. How would a propagandist effectively protect against counter-propaganda?

10. How may hidden or indirect propaganda be used as a persuasion technique?
11. What factors should a propagandist take into account about his audience when attempting to persuade them?
12. What is the significance of Star's and Hughes' research and conclusions regarding advertising campaigns?
13. What conclusions did Scott reach on the effects of role-play on attitude change?
14. Give examples of ethical considerations that should be taken into account in our attempts to change the attitudes and behavior of people around us.
15. Define the following terms: attitude, impression, opinions, reference groups, persuasion, communication process, communicator, message, audience, audience-communicator feedback loop, credibility, sleeper effect, propaganda, counter-propaganda, indirect propaganda, stimulus factors, social background, psychological characteristic, reference groups, role-playing.

ACTION PROJECT 29

Reference Group Survey

Here is a quick way to find out if the students at your school show changes in political attitude similar to that which Newcomb found in his Bennington study. Duplicate the questionnaire below and give it to at least 10 freshmen and 10 seniors. Then convert their ratings into numerical scores. "None" = 1; "little" = 2; and so on. Calculate the average score on Questions 1 and 2 to see if seniors show less similarity to parents and more similarity to other students than do the freshmen. These averages should match the data from Question 4. Question 3 is useful when a student has parents with views similar to those of most students.

STUDENT SURVEY

Please read each question below and mark your answers on the paper with an "X."

1. How much do your social and political views differ from those of your parents?

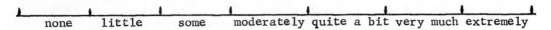

| none | little | some | moderately | quite a bit | very much | extremely |

2. How much do your social and political views differ from the views commonly held by students at this school?

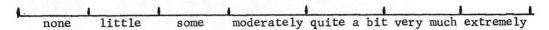

| none | little | some | moderately | quite a bit | very much | extremely |

3. How much do the social and political views of the students at this school differ from the views of your parents?

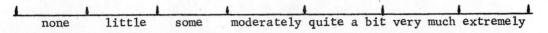

| none | little | some | moderately | quite a bit | very much | extremely |

4. Would you say that your social and political views are closer to those of your parents_____or your fellow students_____?

OUTSIDE READING

Carnegie, Dale. How to Win Friends and Influence People (New York: Simon and Schuster, Inc., 1936; Pocket Books publishes the paperback edition).

Martineau, Pierre. Motivation in Advertising (New York: McGraw-Hill Book Company, Inc., 1957).

McGinnis, Joe. The Selling of the President 1968 (New York: Pocket Books, 1970).

Wrighter, Carl. I Can Sell You Anything (New York: Ballantine Books, Inc., 1972).

Chapter 30

PREDICTING EXAM QUESTIONS

1. Why did the physical sciences develop first and at a faster rate than other forms of science?

2. According to McConnell, what is the future of biological psychology?

3. How may applied psychology involving the use of drugs be of value in the future?

4. Why can we expect greater immediate technological development in biological and behavioral psychology than in intrapsychic psychology?

5. What is the future of applied developmental psychology?

YOUR QUESTIONS

6.

7.

8.

9.

10.

TESTING THE TEST

1. T   F   The ability to control physical objects marked the decline of
            physical technology.
2. T   F   Scientists have within the last few years synthesized a human
            gene in a test tube.
3. T   F   There is a high probability that behavioral scientists will
            work in close conjunction with medical science.
4. T   F   It is likely that some forms of epilepsy will be easily
            treated with conditioning techniques in the near future.
5. T   F   Internal events lend themselves to easy and accurate quanti-
            tative description.
6. T   F   It is highly unlikely that forms of psychological pollution
            will be the focus of change by psychologists in the years to
            come
7. T   F   Psychologists will attempt to teach people to control or
            repress hatred and express their positive feelings more
            openly.
8. T   F   Behavioral engineers will inspect businesses to insure that
            the mental health of employees is a major consideration of
            the employer.
9. T   F   Mental hospitals, as we presently know them, will be virtually
            eliminated.
10. T   F   Prisons based on token economies have a much higher return
            rate than traditional punishment-oriented prisons.

PROVOCATIVE QUESTIONS AND ISSUES

1. What sorts of checks or controls should there be on behavioral
    engineers to prevent some of them from using their power for
    improper or illegal purposes?

CHAPTER OBJECTIVES

1. Describe the future of biological psychology.
2. Give examples of the possible vocations available for psychologists
    in hospital settings.

3. What are the possible uses of biological feedback in curing physical ailments?
4. What are possible future uses of drugs in applied psychology?
5. How will sensory processing be used in applied psychology?
6. What does the future hold for applied intrapsychic and developmental psychology?
7. How will applied psychologists attempt to solve problems of psychological pollution?
8. Give examples of the various forms of treatment which are likely to be available through community mental health centers.
9. Describe the possible vocations for applied psychologists in the field of mass communications.
10. What is the future role of the applied psychologist in industry?
11. Define the following terms: biological psychology, applied hospital psychology, biological feedback, sensory processing, intrapsychic psychology, developmental psychology, psychological pollution, community mental health, mass communication, industrial psychology.

OUTSIDE READING

Brethower, Dale M. Behavioral Analysis in Business and Industry: A Total Performance System (Kalamazoo, Mich.: Behaviordelia, Inc., 1972).

A Career in Psychology. This booklet contains descriptions of specialty areas in psychology, information on how to become a psychologist, and information about the American Psychological Association. It includes an article spotlighting individual professional areas within psychology. Single copies may be obtained free from: Order Department, American Psychological Association, 1200 17th Street N.W., Washington D.C. 20036.

Skinner, B.F. Walden Two (New York: The Macmillan Company, 1948).

Toffler, Alvin. Future Shock (New York: Bantam Books, Inc., 1971).

FEEDBACK REQUEST

How about sending us some feedback about how useful this book has been to you? What are the good points, the things you like most about the Student's Manual?

In what ways could the Student's Manual be improved?

How would you make the improvements?

Other comments or observations:

Please mail this page to: Psychology Editor
College Department
Holt, Rinehart and Winston, Inc.
383 Madison Avenue
New York, New York 10017